DOVER · THRIFT · EDITIONS

Hands Around

A Cycle of Ten Dialogues

ARTHUR SCHNITZLER

DOVER PUBLICATIONS, INC.
New York

DOVER THRIFT EDITIONS

GENERAL EDITOR: STANLEY APPELBAUM
EDITOR OF THIS VOLUME: ALAN WEISSMAN

Copyright

Copyright © 1995 by Dover Publications, Inc.
All rights reserved under Pan American and International Copyright Conventions.

Published in Canada by General Publishing Company, Ltd., 30 Lesmill Road, Don Mills, Toronto, Ontario.
Published in the United Kingdom by Constable and Company, Ltd., 3 The Lanchesters, 162–164 Fulham Palace Road, London W6 9ER.

Theatrical Rights

This Dover Thrift Edition may be used in its entirety, in adaptation or in any other way for theatrical productions and performances, professional and amateur, without fee, permission or acknowledgment.

Bibliographical Note

This Dover edition, first published in 1995, is an unabridged republication of a standard English translation of *Reigen*, which had been first published in German in 1897. A new introductory Note has been specially prepared for this edition.

Library of Congress Cataloging-in-Publication Data

Schnitzler, Arthur, 1862–1931.
  [Reigen. English]
  Hands around : a cycle of ten dialogues / Arthur Schnitzler.
      p.   cm. — (Dover thrift editions)
  ISBN 0-486-28724-6
  I. Title.   II. Series.
PT2638.N5R413   1995
832′.8—dc20   95-22916
                                                                          CIP

Manufactured in the United States of America
Dover Publications, Inc., 31 East 2nd Street, Mineola, N.Y. 11501

Note

Arthur Schnitzler was born in Vienna in 1862, the son of a doctor. He took a medical degree himself and was a practicing physician for years. Increasingly, however, Schnitzler devoted himself to literature, his first love. The drama *Anatol* (1893) established him as a playwright; he also wrote novels — of which *Der Weg ins Freie* (*The Road to the Open*, 1908) is often considered his best — and short stories, of which "Leutnant Gustl" ("Lieutenant Gustl," 1900) and "Fräulein Else" (1924) are two distinguished and well-known examples. "Leutnant Gustl" is one of the earliest examples in any literature of a narrative that consists of a sustained "interior monologue."

Much of Schnitzler's writing mercilessly exposes the decadence of Austrian society in the years prior to the First World War. The present work, *Hands Around* (published in German as *Reigen* ["round dance" or "roundelay"] in 1897), is "A Cycle of Ten Dialogues," each focusing on a sexual liaison. Notable for its frank portrayal of contemporary sexual mores, callousness and hypocrisy, *Hands Around* was considered so explicit in its day that it was not performed until 1920. In that year it was also translated into English, but anonymously, and in its uncut form the translation was circulated only in a small private edition. Finally, in 1950, Schnitzler's play gained wider recognition when it was made into the French film *La Ronde* by Max Ophüls.

Schnitzler's honest, unstinting portrayal of his contemporaries, especially of the military (a sacrosanct institution in Austria), his liberal views and the fact that he was a Jew caused him considerable trouble for many years and made him something of an outcast. Nevertheless, he continued to write uncompromisingly until his death in 1931 in the city where he had been born and whose citizens' flaws he had exposed so ruthlessly.

Arthur Schnitzler has never been as well known in the United States as he has deserved; this Dover Thrift Edition should gain *Hands Around*, an unfairly neglected play, some of the recognition it merits.

Characters

THE GIRL OF THE STREETS
THE SOLDIER
THE PARLOR-MAID
THE YOUNG MAN
THE YOUNG WIFE
THE HUSBAND
THE SWEET YOUNG MISS
THE POET
THE ACTRESS
THE COUNT

The Girl of the Streets and the Soldier

Late in the evening near the Augarten Bridge.

SOLDIER.   (*Enters whistling, on his way home*)

GIRL.   Hello, beautiful boy!

SOLDIER.   (*Turns and goes his way*)

GIRL.   Won't you come with me?

SOLDIER.   Oh, I'm the beautiful boy!

GIRL.   Sure, who else? Do come with me. I live near by.

SOLDIER.   I've no time. I must get back to the barracks.

GIRL.   You'll get to your barracks in time. It's much nicer with me.

SOLDIER.   (*Close to her*) That may be possible.

GIRL.   Ps-st! A guard may pass any minute.

SOLDIER.   Rot! A guard! I carry a saber too!

GIRL.   Ah, come with me.

SOLDIER.   Let me alone. I have no money anyway.

GIRL.   I don't want any money.

SOLDIER.   (*Stopping. They are under a street-lamp*) You don't want any money? What kind of a girl are you, then?

GIRL.   The civilians pay me. Chaps like you don't have to pay me for anything.

SOLDIER.   Maybe you're the girl my pal told me about.

GIRL.   I don't know any pal of yours.

SOLDIER.   You're she, all right! You know — in the café down the street — He went home with you from there.

GIRL.   Lots have gone home with me from that café . . . Oh, lots!

SOLDIER.   All right. Let's go!

GIRL.   So, you're in a hurry now?

SOLDIER.   Well, what are we waiting for? Anyhow, I must be back at the barracks by ten.

GIRL.   Been in service long?

SOLDIER.   What business is that of yours? Is it far?

GIRL.   Ten minutes' walk.

1

SOLDIER.   That's too far for me. Give me a kiss.

GIRL.   (*Kissing him*) I like that best anyway — when I love some one.

SOLDIER.   I don't. No, I can't go with you. It's too far.

GIRL.   Say, come to-morrow afternoon.

SOLDIER.   Sure. Give me your address.

GIRL.   But maybe you won't come.

SOLDIER.   If I promise!

GIRL.   Look here — if my place is too far to-night — there . . . there . . .
   (*She points toward the Danube*)

SOLDIER.   What's there?

GIRL.   It's nice and quiet there, too . . . no one is around.

SOLDIER.   Oh, that's not the real thing.

GIRL.   It's always the real thing with me. Come, stay with me now.
   Who knows, if we'll be alive to-morrow.

SOLDIER.   Come along then — but quick.

GIRL.   Be careful! It's dark here. If you slip, you'll fall in the river.

SOLDIER.   Would be the best thing, perhaps.

GIRL.   Sh-h. Wait a minute. We'll come to a bench soon.

SOLDIER.   You seem to know this place pretty well.

GIRL.   I'd like to have you for a sweetheart.

SOLDIER.   I'd fight too much.

GIRL.   I'd cure you of that soon enough.

SOLDIER.   Humph —

GIRL.   Don't make so much noise. Sometimes a guard stumbles down
   here. Would you believe we are in the middle of Vienna?

SOLDIER.   Come here. Come over here.

GIRL.   You are crazy! If we slipped here, we'd fall into the river.

SOLDIER.   (*Has grabbed her*) Oh you —

GIRL.   Hold tight to me.

SOLDIER.   Don't be afraid . . .

*   *   *

GIRL.   It would have been nicer on the bench.

SOLDIER.   Here or there, it doesn't matter to me . . . Well, pick yourself
   up.

GIRL.   What's your hurry — ?

SOLDIER.   I must get to the barracks. I'll be late anyhow.

GIRL.   Say, what's your name?

SOLDIER.   What's that to you?

GIRL.   My name is Leocadia.

SOLDIER.   Humph! I never heard such a name before.

GIRL.   Listen!

SOLDIER.   Well, what do you want?

GIRL.   Give me just a dime for the janitor.
SOLDIER.   Humph! . . . Do you think I'm your meal-ticket? Good-by,
  Leocadia . . .
GIRL.   Tightwad! Pimp! (*He disappears*)

The Soldier and the Parlor-Maid

Prater Gardens. Sunday Evening. A road which leads from the Wurstelprater[1] into dark tree arcades. Confused music from the Wurstelprater can still be heard; also strains from the cheap dance-hall, a vulgar polka, played by a brass band.

THE SOLDIER.   THE PARLOR-MAID.

MAID.   Now tell me why you wanted to leave.

SOLDIER.   (*Grins sheepishly*)

MAID.   It was so beautiful and I so love to dance.

SOLDIER.   (*Puts his arm around her waist*)

MAID.   (*Submitting*) But we aren't dancing now. Why do you hold me so tight?

SOLDIER.   What's your name? Katy?

MAID.   You've always got a "Katy" on your mind.

SOLDIER.   I know — I know . . . Marie.

MAID.   Goodness, it's dark here. I'm afraid.

SOLDIER.   You needn't be afraid when I'm with you. I can take care of myself!

MAID.   But where are we going? There's no one around. Come, let's go back! . . . It's so dark!

SOLDIER.   (*Pulling at his cigar until it glows brightly*) There . . . it's already getting brighter. Ha — ! Oh, you dearie!

MAID.   Oh! what are you doing there? If I had known this before!

SOLDIER.   The devil take me, if any one at the dance to-day felt softer and rounder than you, Miss Marie.

MAID.   Did you find it out in the same way with all the others?

SOLDIER.   You notice things . . . dancing. You find out lots that way!

MAID.   But you danced much oftener with that cross-eyed blonde than with me.

---

[1] The chief amusement park of Vienna.

4

SOLDIER. She's an old friend of one of my pals.

MAID. Of the corporal with the upturned mustache?

SOLDIER. Oh no, I mean the civilian. You know, the one who was talking with me at the table in the beginning. The one who has such a husky voice.

MAID. Oh I know. He's fresh.

SOLDIER. Did he do anything to you? I'll show him! What did he do to you?

MAID. Oh nothing . . . I only noticed how he was with the others.

SOLDIER. Tell me, Miss Marie . . .

MAID. You'll burn me with your cigar.

SOLDIER. Pardon me! — Miss Marie — or may I say Marie?

MAID. We're not such good friends yet . . .

SOLDIER. There's many who don't like each other, and yet use first names.

MAID. Next time, if we . . . But, Frank!

SOLDIER. Oh, you remember my name?

MAID. But Frank . . .

SOLDIER. That's right, call me Frank, Miss Marie.

MAID. Don't be so fresh — but, sh-h, suppose some one should come!

SOLDIER. What if some one did come? They couldn't see anything two steps off.

MAID. For goodness' sake, where are we going?

SOLDIER. Look! There's two just like us.

MAID. Where? I don't see anything.

SOLDIER. There . . . just ahead of us.

MAID. Why do you say: "two like us" —

SOLDIER. Well, I mean, they like each other too.

MAID. Look out! What's that there? I nearly fell.

SOLDIER. Oh, that's the meadow-gate.

MAID. Don't shove me so. I'll fall.

SOLDIER. Sh-h, not so loud.

MAID. Stop! Now I'm really going to scream — What are you doing? . . . Stop now —

SOLDIER. There's no one anywhere around.

MAID. Then, let's go back where the people are.

SOLDIER. We don't need them. Why — Marie, we need . . . for that . . .

MAID. Stop, Frank, please, for Heaven's sake! Listen to me, if I had . . . known . . . oh . . . come!

*   *   *

SOLDIER. (*Blissfully*) Once more. . . . Oh. . . .

MAID. . . . I can't see your face at all.

SOLDIER.   Don't matter — my face . . .

*   *   *

SOLDIER.   Well, Miss Marie, you can't stay here on the grass all night.
MAID.   Please, Frank, help me.
SOLDIER.   Oh, come along.
MAID.   Oh, Lord help me, Frank.
SOLDIER.   Well, what's the matter with me?
MAID.   You're a bad man, Frank.
SOLDIER.   Yes, yes. Say, wait a minute.
MAID.   Why do you leave me alone?
SOLDIER.   Can't you let me light my cigar!
MAID.   It's so dark.
SOLDIER.   It'll be light again to-morrow morning.
MAID.   Tell me, at least, you love me.
SOLDIER.   Well, you must have felt that, Miss Marie!
MAID.   Where are we going now?
SOLDIER.   Back, of course.
MAID.   Please, don't walk so fast.
SOLDIER.   Well, what's wrong? I don't like to walk around in the dark.
MAID.   Tell me, Frank . . . do you love me?
SOLDIER.   But I just told you that I loved you!
MAID.   Won't you give me a little kiss?
SOLDIER.   (*Condescendingly*) There . . . Listen — There's the music
   again.
MAID.   Would you really like to go back, and dance again?
SOLDIER.   Of course, why not?
MAID.   But, Frank, see, I have to get home. Madame will scold me
   anyway, — she's cranky . . . she'd like it best if I never went out.
SOLDIER.   Well, you can go home.
MAID.   But, I thought, Frank, you'd take me home.
SOLDIER.   Take you home? Oh!
MAID.   Please, it's so sad to go home alone.
SOLDIER.   Where do you live?
MAID.   Not very far — in Porzellanstrasse.
SOLDIER.   So? Then we go the same way . . . but it's still too early for
   me . . . me for the dance . . . I've got late leave to-day . . . I don't need
   to be back at the barracks before twelve o'clock. I'm going to dance.
MAID.   Oh, I see, now it's that cross-eyed blonde's turn.
SOLDIER.   Humph! — Her face isn't so bad.
MAID.   Oh Lord, how wicked men are. I'm sure you do the same to
   every one.

SOLDIER.   That'd be too much! —

MAID.   Please, Frank, no more to-day — stay with me to-day, you see —

SOLDIER.   Oh, very well, all right. But I suppose I may dance.

MAID.   I'm not going to dance with any one else to-night.

SOLDIER.   There it is already . . .

MAID.   What?

SOLDIER.   The hall! How quick we got back. They're still playing the same thing . . . that tatata-tum tatata-tum (*He hums with the band*) . . . Well, I'll take you home, if you want to wait for me . . . if not . . . good-by —

MAID.   Yes, I'll wait. (*They enter the dance-hall*)

SOLDIER.   Say, Miss Marie, get yourself a glass of beer. (*Turning to a blonde who is just dancing past him in the arms of another, very formally*) Miss, may I ask for a dance? —

The Parlor-Maid and the Young Man

Sultry summer afternoon. The parents of the YOUNG MAN *are away in the country. The cook has gone out. The* PARLOR-MAID *is in the kitchen writing a letter to the soldier who is now her sweetheart. The* YOUNG MAN'S *bell rings. She gets up and goes to his room. The* YOUNG MAN *is lying on a couch, smoking a cigarette and reading a French novel.*

MAID.   Yes, Sir?

YOUNG MAN.   Oh, yes, Marie, oh, yes; I rang, yes . . . I only wanted . . . yes, of course . . . Oh, yes, of course, let the blinds down, Marie . . . It's cooler with the blinds down . . . yes . . . (*The* MAID *goes to the window and pulls down the blinds*)

YOUNG MAN.   (*Continues reading*) What are you doing, Marie? Oh, yes. But, now, I can't see to read.

MAID.   You are always so studious, Sir.

YOUNG MAN.   (*Ignoring the remark*) There, that's better. (MAID *goes*)

YOUNG MAN.   (*Tries to go on with his reading, lets the book fall, and rings again*)

MAID.   (*Enters*)

YOUNG MAN.   I say, Marie . . . let's see, what was it I wanted to say? . . . oh, yes . . . Is there any cognac in the house?

MAID.   Yes, but it's locked up.

YOUNG MAN.   Well, who has the key?

MAID.   Lini.

YOUNG MAN.   Who is Lini?

MAID.   The cook, Mr. Alfred.

YOUNG MAN.   Well, then ask Lini for it.

MAID.   Yes, but it's Lini's day out.

YOUNG MAN.   So . . .

MAID.   Can I get anything for you from the café, Sir?

YOUNG MAN.   Thank you, no . . . It is hot enough as it is. I don't nee any cognac. Listen, Marie, bring me a glass of water. Wait, Marie, — let it run, till it gets quite cold.

Exit MAID. *The* YOUNG MAN *gazes after her. At the door the* MAID *looks back at him, and the* YOUNG MAN *glances into the air. The* MAID *turns on the water and lets it run. Meanwhile, she goes into her room, washes her hands, and arranges her curls before the mirror. Then she brings the glass of water to the* YOUNG MAN. *She approaches the couch. The* YOUNG MAN *raises himself upon his elbow. The* MAID *gives him the glass of water and their fingers touch.*

YOUNG MAN.   Thank you — Well, what is the matter? — Be careful. Put the glass back on the tray. (*He leans back, and stretches himself*) How late is it?

MAID.   Five o'clock, Sir.

YOUNG MAN.   Ah, five o'clock. — That's fine. —

MAID.   (*Goes. At the door she turns around. The* YOUNG MAN *has followed her with his eyes; she notices it, and smiles*)

YOUNG MAN.   (*Remains stretched out awhile; then, suddenly, he gets up. He walks to the door, back again, and lies down on the couch. He again tries to read. After a few moments, he rings once more*)

MAID.   (*Appears with a smile which she does not try to hide*)

YOUNG MAN.   Listen, Marie, there was something I wanted to ask you. Didn't Dr. Schueller call this morning?

MAID.   No, Sir, nobody called this morning.

YOUNG MAN.   That is strange. Then, Dr. Schueller didn't call. Do you know Dr. Schueller by sight?

MAID.   Of course, I do. He's the big gentleman with the black beard.

YOUNG MAN.   Yes. Then, perhaps, he called after all?

MAID.   No, Sir. Nobody called.

YOUNG MAN.   (*Resolutely*) Come here, Marie.

MAID.   (*Coming a little nearer*) Yes, Sir.

YOUNG MAN.   Still nearer . . . so . . . ah . . . I only thought . . .

MAID.   Do you want anything, Sir?

YOUNG MAN.   I thought . . . . Well, I thought — only about your blouse . . . what kind of a blouse is it . . . can't you come closer. I won't bite you.

MAID.   (*Comes close to him*) What is the matter with my blouse? Don't you like it, Sir?

YOUNG MAN.   (*Takes hold of her blouse, and draws her down to him*) Blue? It is a nice blue. (*Simply*) You are very prettily dressed, Marie.

MAID.   But, Sir . . .

YOUNG MAN.   Ah . . . What is the matter? . . . (*He has opened her blouse. In a matter of fact tone*) You have a beautiful white skin, Marie.

MAID.   You are flattering me, Sir.

YOUNG MAN.   (*Kissing her on the breast*) That can't hurt you.

MAID.   Oh, no.

YOUNG MAN.   But you sigh so. Why are you sighing?

MAID.   Oh, Mr. Alfred . . .

YOUNG MAN.   And what charming little slippers you have . . .

MAID.   . . . But . . . Sir . . . if the doorbell should ring. —

YOUNG MAN.   Who will ring now?

MAID.   But, Sir . . . look . . . it is so light . . .

YOUNG MAN.   You needn't feel at all shy with me. You needn't feel shy with anybody . . . any one as pretty as you. Yes, really, you are, Marie . . . Do you know your hair actually smells sweet.

MAID.   Mr. Alfred . . .

YOUNG MAN.   Don't make such a fuss, Marie . . . Anyway, I've already seen you otherwise. When I came home the other night and went to get some water, the door to your room was open . . . well . . .

MAID.   (*Covering her face*) Oh, my, I didn't know that Mr. Alfred could be so wicked.

YOUNG MAN.   I *saw* lots then . . . *that* . . . and *that* . . . that . . . and —

MAID.   Oh, Mr. Alfred!

YOUNG MAN.   Come, come . . . here . . . so — that's it . . .

MAID.   But if the doorbell should ring now —

YOUNG MAN.   Now forget that . . . we simply wouldn't open the door.

*   *   *

(*The bell rings*)

YOUNG MAN.   Confound it . . . What a noise that fellow makes — Perhaps he rang before, and we didn't notice it.

MAID.   Oh, no. I was listening all the while.

YOUNG MAN.   Well, see what's the matter. Peek through the curtains.

MAID.   Mr. Alfred . . . you are . . . no . . . such a bad man.

YOUNG MAN.   Please go and see . . . (*Exit* MAID)

YOUNG MAN.   (*Opens the blinds quickly*)

MAID.   (*Returns*) He must have gone away again. Anyway, no one is there now. Perhaps, it was Dr. Schueller.

YOUNG MAN.   (*Annoyed*) Thank you.

MAID.   (*Drawing close to him*)

YOUNG MAN.   (*Evading her*) Listen, Marie, — I'm going to the café now.

MAID.   (*Tenderly*) So soon . . . Mr. Alfred.

YOUNG MAN.   (*Formally*) I am going to the café now . . . If Dr. Schueller should call —

MAID.   He won't come any more to-day.

YOUNG MAN.   (*Severely*) If Dr. Schueller should come, I — I am in the café.

(*He goes to the adjoining room. The* MAID *takes a cigar from the smoking-stand, puts it in her blouse and goes out.*)

The Young Man and the Young Wife

Evening—A drawing-room furnished with cheap elegance in a house in Schwind street. The YOUNG MAN *has just come in; and, still wearing his hat and overcoat, he lights the gas. Then he opens a door to a side-room and looks in. The light from the drawing-room shimmers over the inlaid floor as far as the Louis Quinze bed, which stands against the opposite wall. A reddish light plays from the fire-place in the corner of the bedroom upon the hangings of the bed. The* YOUNG MAN *now inspects the bedroom. He takes an atomizer from the dressing-table, and sprays the bed-pillows with a fine rain of violet perfume. Then he carries the atomizer through both rooms, constantly pressing upon the bulb, so that soon the odor of violets pervades the place. He then takes off his hat and coat. He sits down in a blue velvet armchair, lights a cigarette, and smokes. After a short pause he rises again, and makes sure that the green shutters are closed. Suddenly, he goes into the bedroom, and opens a drawer in the dressing-table. He puts his hand in it, and finds a tortoise-shell hair-pin. He looks for a place to hide it, and finally puts it into a pocket of his overcoat. He opens the buffet in the drawing-room; takes a silver tray, with a bottle and two liqueur glasses, and puts them on the table. He goes back to his overcoat, and takes from it a small white package. Opening this, he places it beside the cognac. He goes again to the buffet, and takes two small plates and knives and forks. He takes a candied chestnut from the package and eats it. Then he pours himself a glass of cognac, and drinks it quickly. He then looks at his watch. He walks up and down the room. He stops a while before a large mirror, ordering his hair and small mustache with a pocket-comb. He next goes to the door of the vestibule and listens. Nothing is stirring. Then he closes the blue portieres, which hang before the bedroom. The bell rings. He starts slightly. Then he sits down in the armchair, and rises only when the door has been opened and the* YOUNG WIFE *enters.*

YOUNG WIFE. (*Heavily veiled, closes the door behind her, pausing a moment with her left hand over her heart, as though mastering a strong emotion*)

YOUNG MAN. (*Goes toward her, takes her left hand, and presses a kiss on the white glove with black stitching. He says softly*) Thank you.

YOUNG WIFE. Alfred — Alfred! YOUNG MAN. Come, Madame ... Come, Emma ...

YOUNG WIFE. Let me be for a minute — please ... oh, please please, Alfred! (*She is still standing at the door*)

YOUNG MAN. (*Standing before her, holding her hand*)

YOUNG WIFE. Where am I?

YOUNG MAN. With me.

YOUNG WIFE. This house is terrible, Alfred.

YOUNG MAN. Why terrible? It is a very proper house.

YOUNG WIFE. But I met two gentlemen on the staircase.

YOUNG MAN. Acquaintances of yours?

YOUNG WIFE. I don't know. It's possible.

YOUNG MAN. But, Madame — You surely know your friends!

YOUNG WIFE. I couldn't see their faces.

YOUNG MAN. But even had they been your best friends — they couldn't possibly have recognized you ... I, myself ... if I didn't know it was you ... this veil —

YOUNG WIFE. There are two.

YOUNG MAN. Won't you come closer? ... And take off your hat, at least?

YOUNG WIFE. What are you thinking of, Alfred? I promised you: Five minutes ... Not a moment more ... I swear it, no more —

YOUNG MAN. Well, then, your veil —

YOUNG WIFE. There are two of them.

YOUNG MAN. Very well, both of them — you will at least let me see your face.

YOUNG WIFE. Do you really love me, Alfred?

YOUNG MAN. (*Deeply hurt*) Emma! You ask me ...

YOUNG WIFE. It's so warm here.

YOUNG MAN. You're still wearing your fur-coat — really, you will catch cold.

YOUNG WIFE. (*Finally enters the room, and throws herself into the armchair*) I'm tired — dead tired.

YOUNG MAN. Permit me. (*He takes off her veil, removes her hat-pin, and puts hat, pin, and veil aside*)

YOUNG WIFE. (*Permits it*)

YOUNG MAN. (*Stands before her, and shakes his head*)

YOUNG WIFE. What is the matter?

YOUNG MAN.   You've never been so beautiful.

YOUNG WIFE.   How is that?

YOUNG MAN.   Alone . . . alone with you — Emma — (*He kneels down
beside her chair, takes both her hands, and covers them with kisses*)

YOUNG WIFE.   And now . . . now let me go again. I have done what you
asked me to do.

YOUNG MAN.   (*Lets his head sink into her lap*)

YOUNG WIFE.   You promised me to be good.

YOUNG MAN.   Yes.

YOUNG WIFE.   It is stifling hot in this room.

YOUNG MAN.   (*Gets up*) You still have your coat on.

YOUNG WIFE.   Put it with my hat.

YOUNG MAN.   (*Takes off her coat, and puts it on the sofa*)

YOUNG WIFE.   And now — good-by —

YOUNG MAN.   Emma — ! Emma — !

YOUNG WIFE.   The five minutes are long past.

YOUNG MAN.   Not one yet! —

YOUNG WIFE.   Alfred, tell me truly now, how late it is.

YOUNG MAN.   It is now exactly a quarter past six.

YOUNG WIFE.   I should have been at my sister's long ago.

YOUNG MAN.   You can see your sister any time . . .

YOUNG WIFE.   Oh, Merciful Heaven, Alfred, why did you tempt me to
come?

YOUNG MAN.   Because . . . I adore you, Emma!

YOUNG WIFE.   To how many have you said the same thing?

YOUNG MAN.   Since I met you, to no one.

YOUNG WIFE.   What a foolish woman I am! If anybody had predicted
. . . just a week ago . . . or even yesterday . . .

YOUNG MAN.   But you had already promised me the day before yesterday.

YOUNG WIFE.   You plagued me so. But I didn't want to do it. God is my
witness — I didn't want to do it . . . Yesterday, I was firmly decided . . .
Do you know I even wrote you a long letter last night?

YOUNG MAN.   I didn't receive any.

YOUNG WIFE.   I tore it up later. Oh, if only I had sent it to you.

YOUNG MAN.   It is better as it is.

YOUNG WIFE.   Oh, no, it's awful . . . of me. I don't understand myself.
Good-by, Alfred, let me go.

YOUNG MAN.   (*Seizes her, and covers her face with burning kisses*)

YOUNG WIFE.   So . . . is that the way you keep your word . . .

YOUNG MAN.   One more kiss — one more.

YOUNG WIFE.   The last. (*He kisses her, and she returns the kiss; their lips
remain joined for a long time*)

YOUNG MAN. Shall I tell you something, Emma? It is now for the first time that I know what happiness is.

YOUNG WIFE. (*Sinks back into the armchair*)

YOUNG MAN. (*Sits on the arm of the chair, and puts one arm lightly about her neck*) . . . or rather, I know now what happiness might be.

YOUNG WIFE. (*Sighs deeply*)

YOUNG MAN. (*Kisses her again*)

YOUNG WIFE. Alfred—Alfred, what are you doing to me!

YOUNG MAN. Wasn't I right?—It isn't so awfully uncomfortable here . . . And we are so safe here. It's a thousand times better than those meetings outdoors . . .

YOUNG WIFE. Oh, don't remind me of them.

YOUNG MAN. I shall always recall them with a thousand delights. Every minute you have let me spend with you is a sweet memory.

YOUNG WIFE. Do you remember the ball at the Manufacturers' Club?

YOUNG MAN. Do I remember it . . . ? I sat beside you through the whole supper—quite close to you. Your husband had champagne . . .

YOUNG WIFE. (*Looks at him with a hurt expression*)

YOUNG MAN. I meant to speak only of the champagne. Emma, would you like a glass of cognac?

YOUNG WIFE. Only a drop, but first give me a glass of water.

YOUNG MAN. Surely . . . But where is—oh, yes, I remember . . . (*He opens the portieres, and goes into the bedroom*)

YOUNG WIFE. (*Follows him with her eyes*)

YOUNG MAN. (*Comes back with a water-bottle and two glasses*)

YOUNG WIFE. Where have you been?

YOUNG MAN. In . . . the adjoining room. (*Pours her a glass of water*)

YOUNG WIFE. Now I'm going to ask you something, Alfred—and you must tell me the truth.

YOUNG MAN. I swear—

YOUNG WIFE. Has there ever been any other woman in these rooms?

YOUNG MAN. But, Emma—this house was built twenty years ago!—

YOUNG WIFE. You know what I mean, Alfred . . . in these rooms, with you!

YOUNG MAN. With me—here—Emma!—It's not kind of you even to imagine such a thing.

YOUNG WIFE. Then there was . . . how shall I . . . But, no, I'd rather not ask. It is better that I shouldn't ask. It's my own fault. Every fault has its punishment.

YOUNG MAN. But what is wrong? What is the matter with you? What fault?

YOUNG WIFE.   No, no, no, I mustn't think . . . Otherwise I would sink through the floor with shame.

YOUNG MAN.   (*With the water-bottle in his hand, shakes his head sadly*) Emma, if you only knew how you hurt me.

YOUNG WIFE.   (*Pours a glass of cognac*)

YOUNG MAN.   I want to tell you something, Emma. If you're ashamed of being here — if you don't care for me — if you don't feel you are all the happiness in the world for me — then you'd better go. —

YOUNG WIFE.   Yes, I shall go.

YOUNG MAN.   (*Taking hold of her hand*) But if you feel that I cannot live without you, that a kiss upon your hand means more to me than all the caresses of all the women in the whole world. . . . Emma, I'm not like other young men, who are experienced in love-making — perhaps, I am too naïve . . . I . . .

YOUNG WIFE.   But suppose you were like other young men?

YOUNG MAN.   Then you wouldn't be here to-night — because you are not like other women.

YOUNG WIFE.   How do you know that?

YOUNG MAN.   (*Drawing her close beside him on the sofa*) I have thought a lot about it. I know you are unhappy.

YOUNG WIFE.   (*Pleased*) Yes.

YOUNG MAN.   Life is so dreary, so empty — and then, — so short — so horribly short! There is only one happiness — to find some one who loves you. —

YOUNG WIFE.   (*Takes a candied pear from the table, and puts it into her mouth*)

YOUNG MAN.   Give me half of it! (*She offers it to him with her lips*)

YOUNG WIFE.   (*Catches the hands of the* YOUNG MAN *that threaten to stray*) What are you doing, Alfred? . . . Is that the way you keep your promise?

YOUNG MAN.   (*Swallows the pear, then, more daringly*) Life is so short.

YOUNG WIFE.   (*Weakly*) But that's no reason —

YOUNG MAN.   (*Mechanically*) Oh, yes.

YOUNG WIFE.   (*Still more weakly*) Alfred, you promised to be good . . . and then it's so light . . .

YOUNG MAN.   Come, come, you only, only . . . (*He lifts her from the sofa*)

YOUNG WIFE.   What are you doing?

YOUNG MAN.   It's not so light in the other room.

YOUNG WIFE.   Is there another room?

YOUNG MAN.   (*Drawing her with him*) A beautiful one . . . and quite dark.

YOUNG WIFE.   We'd better stay in here.

YOUNG MAN.   (*Already past the bedroom portieres with her, loosening her waist*)

YOUNG WIFE.   You are so . . . O merciful Heaven, what are you doing with me! — Alfred!

YOUNG MAN.   I adore you, Emma!

YOUNG WIFE.   So then wait, wait a little . . . (*Weakly*) Go . . . I'll call you.

YOUNG MAN.   Let you help me — let us help you (*becoming confused*) . . . let . . . me — help — you.

YOUNG WIFE.   But you'll tear everything.

YOUNG MAN.   You have no corset on?

YOUNG WIFE.   I never wear a corset. Odilon[1] doesn't wear any either. But you can unbutton my shoes.

YOUNG MAN.   (*Unbuttons her shoes and kisses her feet*)

YOUNG WIFE.   (*Slips into bed*) Oh, how cold it is.

YOUNG MAN.   It'll be warm in a minute.

YOUNG WIFE.   (*Laughing softly*) Do you think so?

YOUNG MAN.   (*Slightly hurt, to himself*) She ought not to have said that. (*He undresses in the dark*)

YOUNG WIFE.   (*Tenderly*) Come, come, come!

YOUNG MAN.   (*Mollified*) In a minute, dear —

YOUNG WIFE.   It smells like violets here.

YOUNG MAN.   That's you . . . Yes (*To her*) you, yourself.

YOUNG WIFE.   Alfred . . . Alfred!!!!

YOUNG MAN.   Emma . . .

*   *   *

YOUNG MAN.   Apparently I love you too much . . . yes . . . I am as if out of my senses.

YOUNG WIFE.   . . .   . . .

YOUNG MAN.   I have been beside myself all these days. I was afraid of this.

YOUNG WIFE.   Don't mind.

YOUNG MAN.   Oh, certainly not. It's perfectly natural, if one . . .

YOUNG WIFE.   No . . . don't . . . You are nervous. Calm yourself first.

YOUNG MAN.   Do you know Stendhal?

YOUNG WIFE.   Stendhal?

YOUNG MAN.   The "Psychologie de l'amour."

YOUNG WIFE.   No. Why do you ask me?

---

[1] A Parisian dancer, famous in the nineties.

YOUNG MAN.   There's a story in that book which is very much to the
  point.
YOUNG WIFE.   What kind of a story?
YOUNG MAN.   There is a gathering of cavalry officers —
YOUNG WIFE.   Yes.
YOUNG MAN.   And they are telling each other about their love affairs.
  And each one of them tells that with the woman he loved best —
  most passionately, you know . . . that with him, that then — well,
  in short, that the same thing happened just as it happened to
  me now.
YOUNG WIFE.   Yes.
YOUNG MAN.   That is very characteristic.
YOUNG WIFE.   Yes.
YOUNG MAN.   The story is not yet ended. One of them maintained . . .
  that this thing had never in his life happened to him, but, adds
  Stendhal — he was known as a great boaster.
YOUNG WIFE.   And. —
YOUNG MAN.   And, yet, it makes you feel blue — that's the stupid side of
  it, even though it's so unimportant.
YOUNG WIFE.   Of course. Anyway, you know . . . you promised me to
  be good.
YOUNG MAN.   Sh-h! Don't laugh. That doesn't help things any.
YOUNG WIFE.   But no, I'm not laughing. That story of Stendhal's is
  really interesting. I have always thought that only older people . . . or
  people who . . . you know, people who have lived fast . . .
YOUNG MAN.   The idea! That has nothing to do with it. By the way, I
  had completely forgotten the prettiest of Stendhal's stories. One of the
  cavalry officers went so far as to say that he stayed for three or even six
  nights . . . I don't remember now — that is he stayed with a woman,
  whom he wanted for weeks — *desirée* — you understand — and nothing happened all those nights except that they wept for happiness . . .
  both . . .
YOUNG WIFE.   Both?
YOUNG MAN.   Yes. Does that surprise you? It seems very compre-
  hensible — especially when two people love each other.
YOUNG WIFE.   But surely there are many who don't weep.
YOUNG MAN.   (*Nervously*) Certainly . . . however, that is an excep-
  tional case.
YOUNG WIFE.   Oh — I thought Stendhal said that all cavalry officers
  weep on such an occasion.
YOUNG MAN.   Look here, now you are laughing at me.
YOUNG WIFE.   What an idea! Don't be childish, Alfred.
YOUNG MAN.   Well, it makes me nervous anyway. . . . Besides I have

the feeling that you are thinking about it all the time. That embarrasses me still more.

YOUNG WIFE. I'm not thinking of it at all.

YOUNG MAN. If I were only sure that you love me.

YOUNG WIFE. Do you want still further proofs?

YOUNG MAN. Didn't I tell you . . . you are always laughing at me.

YOUNG WIFE. How so? Come, let me hold your sweet little head.

YOUNG MAN. Oh, that feels so good.

YOUNG WIFE. Do you love me?

YOUNG MAN. Oh, I'm so happy.

YOUNG WIFE. But you needn't cry about it.

YOUNG MAN. (*Moving away from her, highly irritated*) There! Again! I begged you not to . . .

YOUNG WIFE. To tell you that you shouldn't cry . . .

YOUNG MAN. You said: "You needn't cry about it."

YOUNG WIFE. You are nervous, sweetheart.

YOUNG MAN. I know.

YOUNG WIFE. But you ought not to be. It is beautiful even that . . . that we are together like good comrades . . .

YOUNG MAN. Now you are beginning again.

YOUNG WIFE. Don't you remember! That was one of our first talks. We wanted to be comrades, nothing more. Oh, how nice that was . . . at my sister's ball in January, during the quadrille. . . . For heaven's sake, I should have gone long ago. . . . My sister expects me — what shall I tell her. . . . Good-by, Alfred —

YOUNG MAN. Emma! — You will leave me in this way!

YOUNG WIFE. Yes — so! —

YOUNG MAN. Five minutes more. . . .

YOUNG WIFE. All right. Five minutes more. But you must promise me . . . not to move? . . . Yes? . . . I want to give you a good-by kiss. . . . Psst . . . be still . . . don't move, I told you, otherwise I'll get up at once, you, my sweetheart, sweet . . .

YOUNG MAN. Emma . . . my ador . . . . . .

* * *

YOUNG WIFE. My Alfred!

YOUNG MAN. Oh, it is heaven to be with you.

YOUNG WIFE. But now I've really got to go.

YOUNG MAN. Oh, let your sister wait.

YOUNG WIFE. I must go home. It is much too late to see my sister. How late is it?

YOUNG MAN. How should I know?

YOUNG WIFE. You might look at your watch.

YOUNG MAN.   My watch is in my waistcoat.

YOUNG WIFE.   Get it.

YOUNG MAN.   (*Gets up with a jump*) Eight o'clock.

YOUNG WIFE.   (*Jumps up quickly*) For heaven's sake. . . . Quick, Alfred, give me my stockings. What shall I say? They must be waiting for me at home . . . eight o'clock. . . .

YOUNG MAN.   When shall I see you again?

YOUNG WIFE.   Never.

YOUNG MAN.   Emma! Don't you love me any more?

YOUNG WIFE.   Just for that reason. Give me my shoes.

YOUNG MAN.   Never again? Here are your shoes.

YOUNG WIFE.   My button-hook is in my bag. Please, be quick. . . .

YOUNG MAN.   Here is the button-hook.

YOUNG WIFE.   Alfred, this may cost us our lives.

YOUNG MAN.   (*Unpleasantly moved*) In what way?

YOUNG WIFE.   What shall I say, if he asks me where I've been?

YOUNG MAN.   At your sister's.

YOUNG WIFE.   Oh, if I only could lie.

YOUNG MAN.   Well, you'll have to.

YOUNG WIFE.   Everything for a man like you. Oh, come here . . . let me give you a last kiss. (*She embraces him*) — And now — leave me by myself, go in the other room. — I can't dress, if you are around.

YOUNG MAN.   (*Goes into the drawing-room, where he dresses. He eats some pastry and drinks a glass of cognac*)

YOUNG WIFE.   (*Calls after a while*) Alfred!

YOUNG MAN.   Yes, sweetheart.

YOUNG WIFE.   Isn't it better that we didn't weep?

YOUNG MAN.   (*Smiling, not without pride*) How can you talk so frivolously? —

YOUNG WIFE.   Oh, how difficult it will be now — if we should meet by chance in company?

YOUNG MAN.   By chance? — sometime? . . . Surely you are coming to Lobheimer's to-morrow?

YOUNG WIFE.   Yes. You too?

YOUNG MAN.   Of course. May I ask for the cotillion?

YOUNG WIFE.   Oh, I shall not go. What do you imagine? — I would . . . (*She enters the drawing-room fully dressed, and takes a piece of chocolate pastry*) sink through the floor.

YOUNG MAN.   To-morrow at Lobheimer's. That's fine.

YOUNG WIFE.   No, no . . . I shall decline . . . certainly decline —

YOUNG MAN.   Well, the day after to-morrow . . . here.

YOUNG WIFE.   The idea!

YOUNG MAN.   At six. . . .

YOUNG WIFE.   There are cabs at this corner, aren't there?

YOUNG MAN.   Yes, as many as you want. Well, the day after to-morrow, here at six o'clock. Please say "yes," sweetheart.

YOUNG WIFE.   . . . We'll discuss that to-morrow night during the cotillion.

YOUNG MAN.   (*Embracing her*) My angel.

YOUNG WIFE.   Don't muss my hair again.

YOUNG MAN.   Well then, to-morrow night at Lobheimer's, and the day after to-morrow in my arms.

YOUNG WIFE.   Good-by. . . .

YOUNG MAN.   (*Suddenly anxious again*) And what will you — tell *him* to-night? —

YOUNG WIFE.   Don't ask me . . . don't ask me . . . it's too terrible. — Why do I love you so? — Good-by — If I meet any one again on the stairway, I shall faint. — Ugh!

YOUNG MAN.   (*Kisses her hand for the last time*)

YOUNG WIFE.   (*Exit*)

YOUNG MAN.   (*Remains standing. Then he sits down on the couch. He smiles reflectively, and says to himself*) Now, at last, I have an affair with a respectable woman.

The Young Wife and the Husband

A comfortable bedroom. It is half past ten at night. The WIFE *is lying abed and reading. The* HUSBAND *enters the room in a dressing gown*

YOUNG WIFE.   (*Without looking up*) You have stopped working?

HUSBAND.   Yes. I'm too tired. And besides . . .

YOUNG WIFE.   Well? —

HUSBAND.   I felt so lonely at my desk all at once. A longing for you came over me.

YOUNG WIFE.   (*Looking up*) Really?

HUSBAND.   (*Sitting down on the bed beside her*) Don't read any more to-night. You will ruin your eyes.

YOUNG WIFE.   (*Closing the book*) What's the matter with you?

HUSBAND.   Nothing, child. I'm in love with you. But you know that!

YOUNG WIFE.   One might almost forget it sometimes.

HUSBAND.   One *must* forget it sometimes.

YOUNG WIFE.   Why?

HUSBAND.   Because, otherwise, marriage would be something im-perfect. It would . . . how shall I express it . . . it would lose its sanctity.

YOUNG WIFE.   Oh. . . .

HUSBAND.   Believe me — it is so. . . . If we hadn't sometimes forgotten that we are in love with each other during the five years we have been married — we might not be in love any longer.

YOUNG WIFE.   That's beyond me.

HUSBAND.   The case is simply this. We have had perhaps ten or twelve love-affairs with each other. . . . Doesn't it seem that way to you, too?

YOUNG WIFE.   I haven't counted them!

HUSBAND.   If we had enjoyed the first one to the last drop, if I had from the very beginning surrendered without restraint to my passion for you, the same thing would have happened to us that has happened to millions of other lovers. We would be tired of each other.

YOUNG WIFE.   Ah . . . do you mean that?

USBAND.   Believe me — Emma — in the early days of our marriage, I was afraid that this would happen.

YOUNG WIFE.   I, too.

USBAND.   See? Am I not right? Therefore, it is wise every now and then to live only as good friends.

YOUNG WIFE.   Oh.

USBAND.   And some can always experience new honeymoons, especially since I am careful never to let such weeks of honeymoon . . .

YOUNG WIFE.   Run into months.

USBAND.   That is true.

YOUNG WIFE.   And now . . . now it seems we are at the end of another such period of friendship — ?

USBAND.   (*Pressing her tenderly to him*) So it might seem.

YOUNG WIFE.   But if . . . if I should feel differently?

USBAND.   You couldn't. You are the wisest and most delicious being in the world. I am very happy to have found you.

YOUNG WIFE.   You know how to make love very well — every now and then.

USBAND.   (*Who has also gone to bed*) Well, for a man who has looked about in the world a bit — come, lay your head on my shoulder — who has seen something of the world, marriage is really something much more mysterious than it is for you sheltered young girls. You come to us entirely innocent and . . . to a certain degree, at least, ignorant of things, and therefore you really understand the essence of love much better than we.

YOUNG WIFE.   (*Laughing*) Oh!

USBAND.   Certainly. For we get all tangled up by the many experiences that we have to go through before marriage. You women, of course, hear a lot of things, you know a lot of things, no doubt read too much, but you can't have any real idea of the things men experience. We men really become quite disgusted with this thing people call love, for the kind of creatures to which we are restricted really are. . . .

YOUNG WIFE.   Tell me — what kind of creatures are they?

USBAND.   (*Kissing her on the forehead*) You ought to be glad, dear child, that you never have had a glimpse of relations like that. After all most of the poor things deserve pity — it is not for us to throw stones.

YOUNG WIFE.   But — this pity — it doesn't seem quite appropriate to me.

USBAND.   (*With gentle benevolence*) They deserve it. You young girls of good family, who wait quietly under the care of your parents for the man who desires you in marriage, — you won't know the misery that drives most of these poor creatures into the arms of sin.

YOUNG WIFE.   Do all of them really sell themselves?

HUSBAND.   I would hardly say that. I don't mean the material mise
    alone. There is also — one might call it — a moral misery, a lack
    appreciation for what is permissible, and, especially, for what is nob

YOUNG WIFE.   But why are they to be pitied? — They seem to enj
    themselves.

HUSBAND.   You have strange ideas, my child. You must not forget th
    such people are predestined by nature to sink lower and lower. The
    is no stopping them.

YOUNG WIFE.   (*Cuddling to him*) It seems pleasant to fall.

HUSBAND.   (*Hurt*) How can you say things like that, Emma? I shou
    think that to good women like you, nothing could be more repulsi
    than those who are not!

YOUNG WIFE.   Of course, Karl, of course. I was just thinking. Go o
    tell me more. I like it when you talk like this. Tell me somethin

HUSBAND.   What? —

YOUNG WIFE.   Why — about these people.

HUSBAND.   The idea!

YOUNG WIFE.   But, I asked you a long time ago — you know, when v
    were first married to tell me something of your younger days.

HUSBAND.   Why does that interest you?

YOUNG WIFE.   Aren't you my husband? Isn't it a sort of injustice tha
    really know nothing about your past?

HUSBAND.   You surely don't think I have such bad taste, as to — N
    Emma . . . it would be like a profanation.

YOUNG WIFE.   And yet you have . . . heaven knows how many oth
    women you have held in your arms, just as you are holding me no

HUSBAND.   Don't say "women." You are *the* woman.

YOUNG WIFE.   But you must answer one question . . . otherwise .
    otherwise . . . there won't be any honeymoon.

HUSBAND.   That's a nice way to talk . . . remember you are a moth
    . . . our little girl is sleeping in there. . . .

YOUNG WIFE.   (*Snuggling against him*) But I want a boy, too.

HUSBAND.   Emma!

YOUNG WIFE.   Don't be silly . . . of course, I am your wife . . . but
    like also to be . . . to be your sweetheart.

HUSBAND.   Would you? . . .

YOUNG WIFE.   Well — now my question.

HUSBAND.   (*Accommodating*) All right.

YOUNG WIFE.   Was there . . . a married woman . . . amongst the

HUSBAND.   Why? What do you mean?

YOUNG WIFE.   You know what I mean.

HUSBAND.   (*Slightly disconcerted*) What makes you think of a thi
    like that?

YOUNG WIFE. I would like to know if . . . I mean — there are such women. . . . I know that very well. But did you? . . .

HUSBAND. (*Seriously*) Do you know such a woman?

YOUNG WIFE. Well, I hardly know.

HUSBAND. Is there, perhaps, such a woman among your friends?

YOUNG WIFE. How can I be sure that there is — or that there isn't?

HUSBAND. Did any of your friends . . . women talk about a lot of things — alone among themselves — did any of them ever confess — ?

YOUNG WIFE. (*Uncertainly*) No.

HUSBAND. Do you suspect any of your friends — that she . . .

YOUNG WIFE. Suspect . . . oh . . . suspect.

HUSBAND. It would seem so.

YOUNG WIFE. No, indeed, Karl, most certainly not. When I think things over — I don't believe there is any one.

HUSBAND. No one?

YOUNG WIFE. Not among my friends.

HUSBAND. Promise me something, Emma.

YOUNG WIFE. Well?

HUSBAND. That you will never associate with a woman about whom you have the slightest suspicion that she . . . doesn't lead a completely blameless life.

YOUNG WIFE. And you think it necessary for me to promise that?

HUSBAND. I know that you will not seek out the company of such women. But, it might happen that you . . . in fact it often happens that such women, whose reputations are not of the best, seek out good women, partly to give them standing, and partly because they feel . . . how shall I say? . . . because they feel a certain homesickness for virtue.

YOUNG WIFE. Do they?

HUSBAND. Yes. I believe what I just said is very true. Homesickness for virtue. For all of these women are at heart very unhappy; you can believe that.

YOUNG WIFE. Why?

HUSBAND. You ask me, Emma? — How can you even ask? — Just imagine what a life these women lead! Full of lies, perfidy, vulgarity, and danger.

YOUNG WIFE. Yes, of course. You are right.

HUSBAND. Truly . . . they pay for their little happiness . . . their little . . .

YOUNG WIFE. Pleasure.

HUSBAND. Why "pleasure"? Why do you call it "pleasure"?

YOUNG WIFE. Well, — there must be something in it — ! Otherwise, they wouldn't do it.

HUSBAND.   It is nothing . . . an intoxication.

YOUNG WIFE.   (*Pensively*) An intoxication . . .

HUSBAND.   No, it is not even intoxication. Like everything — it is dearly paid for, that much is certain.

YOUNG WIFE.   Well . . . it has happened to you, hasn't it?

HUSBAND.   Yes, Emma. — And it is the thing I most regret.

YOUNG WIFE.   Who was she? Tell me! Do I know her?

HUSBAND.   The idea!

YOUNG WIFE.   Was it long ago? Was it very long before you married me?

HUSBAND.   Don't ask me. Please, don't ask.

YOUNG WIFE.   But, Karl!

HUSBAND.   She is dead.

YOUNG WIFE.   Are you in earnest?

HUSBAND.   Yes . . . it sounds almost ridiculous, but I have the feeling that all such women die young.

YOUNG WIFE.   Did you love her very much?

HUSBAND.   One doesn't love women who lie.

YOUNG WIFE.   Then why . . .

HUSBAND.   An intoxication. . . .

YOUNG WIFE.   Really?

HUSBAND.   Don't talk about it any more, please. All that is passed long ago. I have only loved one woman — that is you. You only love where there is purity and truth.

YOUNG WIFE.   Karl!

HUSBAND.   Oh, how secure, how happy one feels in such arms. Why didn't I know you as a child? I am sure I wouldn't then even have looked at other women.

YOUNG WIFE.   Karl!

HUSBAND.   And how beautiful you are! . . . beautiful! . . . Oh, come. . . . (*He puts the light out*)

*   *   *

YOUNG WIFE.   Do you know what I am thinking of to-night?

HUSBAND.   What, sweetheart?

YOUNG WIFE.   Of . . . of . . . of Venice.

HUSBAND.   Our first night. . . .

YOUNG WIFE.   Yes. . . .

HUSBAND.   What then? Tell me!

YOUNG WIFE.   You love me as much to-day.

HUSBAND.   Yes, just as much.

YOUNG WIFE.   Oh . . . if you would always . . .

HUSBAND.   (*In her arms*) If I would what?

YOUNG WIFE.   My Karl!

HUSBAND.   What do you mean? If I would always? . . .

YOUNG WIFE.   Well, yes.

HUSBAND.   Well, what then, if I would always? . . .

YOUNG WIFE.   Then I would always know that you love me.

HUSBAND.   Yes. But you must know that anyway. One cannot always be a lover, sometimes one has to go out into the cold world to struggle and achieve! Don't forget that, my child. There is a time for everything in marriage — that is the beauty of it. There are not many who can remember their Venice after five years.

YOUNG WIFE.   True!

HUSBAND.   And now . . . good-night, my child.

YOUNG WIFE.   Good-night!

The Husband and the Sweet Young Miss

A private dining-room in the Riedhof, comfortably furnished with moderately good taste. A gas-grate is burning. The HUSBAND *and the* SWEET YOUNG MISS *are disclosed. The remains of dinner are on the table, cream-cakes, fruit, cheese. In the wine-glasses is a Hungarian white wine.*

HUSBAND. (*Is smoking a Havana cigar, and leaning against the corner of a sofa*)

MISS. (*Sits beside him in an armchair, eating the cream out of a cake with a spoon, and tasting it with satisfaction*)

HUSBAND. Is it good?

MISS. (*Without stopping*) Oh!

HUSBAND. Do you want another?

MISS. No. I've eaten too much already.

HUSBAND. Your wine is all gone. (*He fills her glass*)

MISS. No . . . stop. I'll leave it anyway.

HUSBAND. Why are you so shy?

MISS. Am I? — Well, it takes time to get acquainted.

HUSBAND. Come and sit here with me.

MISS. Right away. . . . I'm not ready yet.

HUSBAND. (*Rises and stands behind her chair, and puts his arms around her, turning her face toward him*)

MISS. What's the matter?

HUSBAND. I want a kiss.

MISS. (*Kissing him*) You are . . . excuse me, you have a lot of nerve.

HUSBAND. You're just finding that out?

MISS. Oh, no, I knew that long ago . . . from the first, in the street. — You must —

HUSBAND. What?

MISS. You must have a nice opinion of me.

HUSBAND. Why?

MISS. Because I went right away with you to a private dining-room

28

HUSBAND.   Well, you can hardly say "right away."

MISS.   But you asked in such a nice way.

HUSBAND.   Do you think so?

MISS.   And, after all, what is the harm?

HUSBAND.   Of course.

MISS.   Whether we go walking or —

HUSBAND.   Besides, it's much too cold for walking.

MISS.   Yes, it was too cold.

HUSBAND.   But here it's nice and warm, isn't it? (*He sits down again, puts his arms around the girl, and draws her to his side*)

MISS.   (*Weakly*) Don't.

HUSBAND.   Tell me. . . . You noticed me before, didn't you?

MISS.   Certainly. Several blocks before you spoke to me.

HUSBAND.   I don't mean to-day. I mean yesterday and the day before, when I was following you.

MISS.   A lot of people follow me.

HUSBAND.   I don't doubt that. But did you notice me?

MISS.   Guess . . . do you know what happened to me the other day? My cousin's husband followed me in the dark, and didn't recognize me.

HUSBAND.   Did he speak to you?

MISS.   What do you suppose? Do you imagine every one is as bold as you?

HUSBAND.   But they sometimes do, don't they?

MISS.   Of course, they do.

HUSBAND.   Well, and what do you do?

MISS.   Why nothing — I just don't answer.

HUSBAND.   Hm-m . . . but you answered me.

MISS.   Are you sorry?

HUSBAND.   (*Kisses her violently*) Your lips taste like cream-cakes.

MISS.   Oh, they are sweet by nature.

HUSBAND.   I suppose many have told you that?

MISS.   Many! What are you dreaming of?

HUSBAND.   Now, be honest. How many have kissed this mouth before?

MISS.   Why do you ask? You wouldn't believe me anyhow, if I told you.

HUSBAND.   Why not?

MISS.   Guess, then.

HUSBAND.   All right, I'll guess — but you mustn't get angry!

MISS.   Why should I get angry?

HUSBAND.   Well, then, I'll guess . . . twenty.

MISS.   (*Slipping away from him*) So — why not make it a hundred?

HUSBAND.   Oh, I was just guessing.

MISS.   You guessed badly.

HUSBAND.   Say — ten.

MISS.   (*Offended*) Oh, of course. A girl who lets a man talk to her on the street, and goes right away with him to a private dining-room!

HUSBAND.   Don't be childish. Whether we walk about in the streets or sit in a room. . . . We are in a restaurant. The waiter may come in at any moment — it doesn't signify anything at all. . . .

MISS.   That's just what I thought.

HUSBAND.   Have you ever been in a private dining-room before?

MISS.   If I must tell the truth — yes.

HUSBAND.   I am glad that you are honest with me at least.

MISS.   But it wasn't — no it wasn't the way you imagine. I was in a private dining-room with a friend and her fiancé, once during the carnival.

HUSBAND.   It wouldn't have been anything tragic, if you had even gone — with your sweetheart —

MISS.   Of course, it wouldn't have been anything serious. But I haven't any sweetheart.

HUSBAND.   Oh, come now.

MISS.   I swear, I haven't.

HUSBAND.   But you don't expect to make me believe that I . . .

MISS.   Make you believe what? . . . I haven't any — at least, haven't had for six months.

HUSBAND.   I see. . . . But before then? Who was he?

MISS.   Why are you so curious?

HUSBAND.   I am curious because I love you.

MISS.   Really?

HUSBAND.   Of course! You should have noticed that. Tell me about him. (*Presses her tightly to him*)

MISS.   What do you want me to tell?

HUSBAND.   Don't keep me in suspense so long. Who was he, that's what I want to know.

MISS.   (*Laughing*) Just a man.

HUSBAND.   Well — well — who?

MISS.   He looked something like you.

HUSBAND.   No!

MISS.   If you hadn't looked so much like him —

HUSBAND.   Well, what then?

MISS.   Now, don't ask, don't you see that . . .

HUSBAND.   (*Understanding*) That's why you let me speak to you.

MISS.   Yes, that's it.

HUSBAND.   I really don't know whether I ought to be pleased or angry.

MISS.   If I were you, I'd be pleased.

HUSBAND.   All right.

MISS.   You also remind me of him the way you speak . . . and the way you look at one. . . .

HUSBAND.   What was he?

MISS.   And then, the eyes —

HUSBAND.   What was his name?

MISS.   Please don't look at me that way; please don't.

HUSBAND.   (*Embraces her. A long, burning kiss*)

MISS.   (*Trembles, and tries to get up*)

HUSBAND.   Why do you want to leave me?

MISS.   It's time to go home.

HUSBAND.   Later.

MISS.   No, I really have to get home. What do you think mother will say.

HUSBAND.   You live with your mother?

MISS.   Of course, I live with my mother. What did you imagine?

HUSBAND.   So — with your mother. Do you live alone with her?

MISS.   Oh, yes, alone! There are five of us! Two boys and two more girls.

HUSBAND.   Don't sit so far away from me. Are you the oldest?

MISS.   No, I'm the second. First comes Kitty. She's working in a flower store. Then come I.

HUSBAND.   Where do you work?

MISS.   I stay at home.

HUSBAND.   Always?

MISS.   One of us has to stay home.

HUSBAND.   Of course, — and what do you tell your mother, when you — come home so late?

MISS.   That happens so seldom.

HUSBAND.   Well, to-day, for example. Your mother will ask you, won't she?

MISS.   Of course, she'll ask. It doesn't matter how careful I am when I come home, she always wakes up.

HUSBAND.   And what do you tell her?

MISS.   Oh — that I've been to the theater.

HUSBAND.   Does she believe that?

MISS.   Why shouldn't she believe it? I often go to the theater. I saw an opera on Sunday with my friend and her fiancé, and my oldest brother.

HUSBAND.   Where did you get the tickets?

MISS.   My brother is a hairdresser.

HUSBAND.   Oh, yes, a hairdresser . . . at the theater, I suppose?

MISS.   Why are you asking so many questions?

HUSBAND.   Because I am interested. What does your other brother do?

MISS.   He's still going to school. He wants to become a teacher. Just imagine!

HUSBAND.   And you also have a little sister?

MISS.   Yes, she is a mere child, but you have to keep an eye on her all the time already. You have no idea how girls are spoiled at school. Just imagine! The other day I caught her keeping a date.

HUSBAND.   Really?

MISS.   Yes! She was out walking one evening at half-past seven with a boy from the school across the way. A mere child like her!

HUSBAND.   And what did you do?

MISS.   I gave her a spanking.

HUSBAND.   Are you as strict as all that?

MISS.   Well, who would be if I wasn't? My older sister is working and mother does nothing but grumble — everything always depends on me.

HUSBAND.   You are a dear, sweet girl! (*Kisses her, and grows more tender*) You also remind me of some one.

MISS.   So — of whom?

HUSBAND.   Of no one in particular . . . of bygone days . . . of my youth. Come, drink, child!

MISS.   How old are you? . . . You . . . why . . . I don't even know your name.

HUSBAND.   Karl.

MISS.   Is it possible? Your name is Karl?

HUSBAND.   Was his name also Karl?

MISS.   No, but that's the queer thing . . . that is . . . the eyes. . . . (*shaking her head*) the way you look at me. . . .

HUSBAND.   And who was he? — You haven't told me yet.

MISS.   Oh, he was a bad man — that's sure, otherwise he wouldn't have gone away.

HUSBAND.   Did you love him very much?

MISS.   Of course, I loved him.

HUSBAND.   I know what he was — a lieutenant.

MISS.   No, he wasn't in the army. He couldn't pass the examinations. His father owns a house in . . . but why do you have to know?

HUSBAND.   (*Kisses her*) You have gray eyes. I thought, at first, they were black.

MISS.   Well aren't they pretty enough?

HUSBAND.   (*Kisses her eyes*)

MISS.   Don't please — I can't bear it. . . . O, please don't . . . let me get up . . . only for a moment — please.

HUSBAND.   (*More tenderly still*) No, indeed.

MISS.   But, please, Karl. . . .

HUSBAND.   How old are you? — eighteen — isn't it?

MISS.   Just past nineteen.

HUSBAND.   Nineteen . . . and I —

MISS.   You are thirty. . . .

HUSBAND.   And a little more — Don't let's talk about it.

MISS.   He was thirty-two, when I first met him.

HUSBAND.   How long ago was that?

MISS.   I don't remember. . . . Listen, there must have been something in the wine.

HUSBAND.   What makes you think so?

MISS.   I am quite . . . see — everything is turning round about me.

HUSBAND.   Then hold tight to me. So. . . . (*He holds her close to him, and becomes more and more tender. She hardly resists*) I'll tell you something, dear, we might go now.

MISS.   Yes . . . home.

HUSBAND.   Well, not exactly home. . . .

MISS.   What do you mean? . . . O, no — no. . . . I won't go anywhere else. What do you think I am?

HUSBAND.   But listen to me, child — the next time we meet, you know, we will arrange it so that . . . (*He has slipped to the floor with his head in her lap*) This is so comfy, oh, so comfy!

MISS.   What are you doing? (*She kisses his hair*) Something must have been in that wine — I'm so sleepy . . . what would happen, if I couldn't get up again? But, but — look, but Karl . . . if some one should come in . . . please . . . the waiter.

HUSBAND.   No . . . waiter . . . will ever come in . . . here. . . .

*   *   *

MISS.   (*Leaning with closed eyes in the corner of the sofa*)

HUSBAND.   (*Pacing up and down the little room, after having lighted a cigarette*) (*Long silence*)

HUSBAND.   (*Looking for a long time at the girl; speaking to himself*) Who knows what sort of a person she really is — Confound it . . . so quickly . . . that wasn't very cautious of me . . . hm-m. . . .

MISS.   (*Without opening her eyes*) There must have been something in the wine.

HUSBAND.   Why?

MISS.   Otherwise. . . .

HUSBAND.   Why do you blame everything on the wine? . . .

MISS.   Where are you? Why do you stay so far away? Come to me.

HUSBAND.   (*Sits beside her*)

MISS.   Now tell me if you really love me.

HUSBAND. But you know that . . . (*He interrupts himself quickly*) Of course.

MISS. Listen. . . . There must have . . . come, tell me the truth, what was in the wine.

HUSBAND. Well, do you think I . . . I would drug your wine?

MISS. Well, see, I can't understand it. I'm really not that kind. . . . We've known each other only since . . . Dear, I'm not that kind . . . honestly, I'm not — if you think that of me —

HUSBAND. Well — why worry about that? I don't think anything bad of you. I only think that you love me.

MISS. Yes. . . .

HUSBAND. After all, when two young people are alone in a room, and have dinner, and drink wine . . . there doesn't need to be anything in the wine.

MISS. I merely said it to say something.

HUSBAND. But, why?

MISS. (*Almost defiantly*) Because I was ashamed.

HUSBAND. How absurd! There is no reason to be. Especially, since I made you think of your first sweetheart.

MISS. Yes.

HUSBAND. Your *first* sweetheart.

MISS. Yes, yes. . . .

HUSBAND. Now I should like to know who the others were.

MISS. There weren't any.

HUSBAND. That is not true, it can't be true.

MISS. Oh, please, don't tease me.

HUSBAND. Would you like a cigarette?

MISS. No, thanks.

HUSBAND. Do you know how late it is?

MISS. Well?

HUSBAND. Half-past eleven.

MISS. Really?

HUSBAND. Well . . . and your mother? She's used to this, is she?

MISS. Do you really want to send me home?

HUSBAND. But earlier in the evening you yourself wanted —

MISS. You are quite changed. What have I done to you?

HUSBAND. But, child, what is the matter with you, what do you imagine?

MISS. And it was only your looks, believe me, or you would have had to wait . . . many men have asked me to go with them to a private dining-room.

HUSBAND. Well, would you like . . . to come here again with me soon . . . or rather somewhere else?

MISS.   I don't know.

HUSBAND.   What do you mean by, "I don't know"?

MISS.   Well, why don't you make a date?

HUSBAND.   When? First of all, I must explain that I do not live in Vienna. I am only here for a few days' visit now and then.

MISS.   Oh, you're not a Viennese?

HUSBAND.   Yes, I am a Viennese. But I am living out of town now. . . .

MISS.   Where?

HUSBAND.   Oh, well, that doesn't matter.

MISS.   Oh, don't be frightened, I won't come to see you.

HUSBAND.   If it would give you any pleasure you may come. I live in Graz.

MISS.   Honestly?

HUSBAND.   Yes, why does that surprise you?

MISS.   You are married, aren't you?

HUSBAND.   (*Greatly surprised*) What makes you think that?

MISS.   I just got the impression.

HUSBAND.   And you wouldn't mind that at all?

MISS.   Well, I would rather that you were single.—So you are married!—

HUSBAND.   But, tell me first what made you think of that?

MISS.   If a man says he doesn't live in Vienna, and he doesn't always have time—

HUSBAND.   But that's not so improbable.

MISS.   I don't believe it.

HUSBAND.   And wouldn't it hurt your conscience to have caused a married man to become unfaithful?

MISS.   Oh, my, no doubt your wife acts just like you.

HUSBAND.   (*Very indignant*) That will do. No more of such remarks.

MISS.   I thought you didn't have a wife.

HUSBAND.   Whether I have one or not—such remarks are uncalled for. (*He has risen*)

MISS.   But Karl, Karl, what is the matter? Are you angry? I really didn't know that you were married. I was just talking. Come, don't be angry.

HUSBAND.   (*Comes back to her after a few minutes*) You are strange creatures, you . . . women. (*He becomes tender again*)

MISS.   Stop . . . don't . . . it's too late now.

HUSBAND.   Well, listen to me a minute. Let's talk seriously. I would like to see you again, to see you often.

MISS.   Would you?

HUSBAND.   But one thing is necessary . . . that I can depend upon you. I can't look out for you.

MISS.   Oh, I can look out for myself.

HUSBAND.   You are . . . well, I can't just say inexperienced — but, you are young — and — men in general are pretty unscrupulous.

MISS.   Oh, my!

HUSBAND.   I don't mean on the moral side only. — Well, you know what I mean —

MISS.   Tell me, what do you think I am?

HUSBAND.   Look here — if you want me — me only — we can easily arrange it — even if I do generally live in Graz. In a place like this where some one may come in at any moment, it isn't very comfortable.

MISS.   (*Snuggles up to him*)

HUSBAND.   Next time . . . we shall go somewhere else, won't we?

MISS.   Yes.

HUSBAND.   Where we may be entirely alone.

MISS.   Yes.

HUSBAND.   (*Embracing her passionately*) We'll discuss the rest on the way home. (*He rises, and opens the door*) Waiter . . . the bill!

The Sweet Young Miss and the Poet

A small room, furnished with taste and comfort. Red curtains half-darken the room. A large writing-table strewn with books and papers. A piano against the wall. The SWEET YOUNG MISS *and the* POET *are disclosed. They are just entering. The* POET *closes the door.*

POET.   (*Kisses her*) My darling!

MISS.   (*With hat and coat*) Oh! It's very pretty here! Only you can't see anything!

POET.   Your eyes will have to get used to this semi-darkness. — Those sweet eyes — (*Kisses her eyes*)

MISS.   But there won't be time enough.

POET.   Why not?

MISS.   Because I can only stop a moment.

POET.   But, you can take your hat off, can't you?

MISS.   Just for the sake of a minute?

POET.   (*Takes the pin out of her hat which he removes*) And your coat —

MISS.   The idea! — I have to leave right away.

POET.   But you must rest a while first. We have been walking for three hours.

MISS.   Riding, you mean.

POET.   Yes, we rode home — but we ran around for a full three hours in the country. Now come, sit down, child . . . wherever you like — here at my desk; — no, that's not comfortable. Sit down on the sofa. — That's it. (*He presses her down*) If you are very tired, you may as well lie down. So. (*He stretches her out on the sofa*) There, put your head on the cushion.

MISS.   (*Laughing*) But I'm not tired at all!

POET.   You merely imagine you're not. So — and if you are sleepy, you can go to sleep. I shall be very quiet. And what's more I can play you a lullaby . . . one of my own. . . . (*He goes to the piano*)

MISS.   One of yours.

POET.   Yes.

MISS. But I thought, Robert, you were a professor.

POET. I? But I told you I was a writer. But what made you think of that?

MISS. Because you said the piece you are playing is your own.

POET. Yes . . . perhaps it is, perhaps it isn't. But that doesn't matter. Well? Anyway it doesn't matter who composed it, if only it is beautiful. Don't you agree?

MISS. Of course . . . it must be beautiful . . . that's the chief thing! —

POET. Do you know what I meant by that?

MISS. By what?

POET. By what I just said.

MISS. (*Sleepily*) Of course I do.

POET. (*Gets up, goes to her, and strokes her hair*) You didn't understand a word.

MISS. I'm not as stupid as that.

POET. Certainly you are, but that is just the reason why I love you. It is so beautiful, when girls are stupid. I mean in the way you are.

MISS. Go on, you are talking nonsense.

POET. Angel, little one! Isn't it comfy on this soft, Persian couch cover?

MISS. Indeed, it is. Won't you play something else on the piano?

POET. No, I'd rather stay near you. (*Caressing her*)

MISS. But hadn't you better light the lamp?

POET. Oh, no. . . . The dim light is so restful. We were as if bathed in sunbeams all day. Now we've just climbed out of the bath and slipped on . . . the twilight like a bathrobe — (*laughs*) No — that ought to be expressed differently. . . . Don't you think so?

MISS. I don't know.

POET. (*Moves slightly away from her*) Absolutely divine, this stupidity. (*He takes out a notebook, and writes a few words in it*)

MISS. What are you doing? (*She turns toward him*) What are you writing?

POET. (*Softly*) Sun, bath, twilight, cloak . . . so . . . (*He puts the notebook back. Aloud*) Nothing. . . . Now tell me, sweetheart, wouldn't you like something to eat or drink?

MISS. I'm not thirsty, but I am hungry.

POET. Hm . . . it would suit me better, if you were thirsty. I have some cognac at home, but I have to send out for food.

MISS. Can't you send somebody?

POET. That is difficult, my servant isn't here now — but, wait a minute — I will go myself . . . what would you like?

MISS. Oh, really don't bother; I have to go home anyway.

POET. Child, that's out of the question. Now I will tell you something, when we leave, we will go together somewhere for supper.

MISS. Oh, no. I haven't time for that. And, then, where could we go? Somebody we know might see us.

POET. Do you know such a lot of people?

MISS. Well, it takes only one to make trouble for us.

POET. Why trouble?

MISS. Well, suppose mother should hear about it. . . .

POET. We can go somewhere, where no one can see us. There are plenty of restaurants with private dining-rooms.

MISS. (*Singing*) "Let's dine in a chambre separée!"

POET. Have you ever been in a private dining-room?

MISS. To tell the truth — yes.

POET. Who was the happy man?

MISS. Oh, it wasn't the way you imagine. . . . I went with a friend and her fiancé. They took me along.

POET. And you expect me to believe that?

MISS. You needn't believe it!

POET. (*Close to her*) Did you blush? You can hardly see anything. I can't even distinguish your features. (*He touches her cheeks with his hands*) But even so I recognize you.

MISS. Well, be careful that you don't take me for some one else.

POET. It is strange, I don't seem to remember how you look.

MISS. Thank you!

POET. (*Seriously*) It is almost uncanny. I can't imagine any longer how you look — In a certain way I have already forgotten you — Now, if I couldn't remember even the sound of your voice . . . what would you do then? — Something near and far away at the same time . . . it's uncanny.

MISS. What are you talking about?

POET. Nothing, my angel, nothing. Where are your lips? . . . (*He kisses her*)

MISS. Wouldn't it be better to light the lamp?

POET. No. . . . (*Very tenderly*) Tell me, do you love me?

MISS. Very much . . . oh, so much!

POET. Have you ever loved any one as much as me?

MISS. I told you already that I didn't.

POET. But . . . (*He sighs*)

MISS. He was my fiancé.

POET. I'd rather you wouldn't think of him now.

MISS. Why . . . what's the difference . . . look. . . .

POET. We might imagine now that we were in a palace in India.

MISS. I'm sure people there wouldn't be as wicked as you are.

POET. How idiotic! Perfectly divine — Ah, if you only know what you are to me. . . .

MISS. Well?

POET. Don't always push me away, I'm not going to hurt you —

MISS. My corset hurts me.

POET. (*Simply*) Take it off.

MISS. Yes. But you must behave.

POET. Of course!

MISS. (*Rises, and takes off her corset in the darkness*)

POET. (*Sits in the meantime on the sofa*) Tell me, aren't you at all curious to know my name?

MISS. Yes, what is it?

POET. I'd rather not tell you my real name, but the name I go by.

MISS. What is the difference?

POET. I mean the name I use as a writer.

MISS. Oh, you don't write under your real name?

POET. (*Close to her*)

MISS. Oh . . . stop . . . don't.

POET. What fragrance! How sweet. (*He kisses her breasts*)

MISS. You are tearing my chemise.

POET. Away with it . . . away with it . . . everything is superfluous.

MISS. Oh, Robert.

POET. And now enter into our Indian palace.

MISS. Tell me first — do you really love me?

POET. I adore you. (*Kisses her passionately*) I adore you, my sweetheart, my springtime . . . my . . .

MISS. Robert . . . Robert. . . .

*　　*　　*

POET. It was heaven. . . . My name is . . .

MISS. Robert — oh, my Robert!

POET. I call myself Biebitz.

MISS. Why do you call yourself Biebitz?

POET. My name is not Biebitz — I just use it as a pseudonym . . . well, don't you recognize the name?

MISS. No.

POET. You don't know the name Biebitz? Ah — Perfectly divine! Really? You are just pretending you don't know it, aren't you?

MISS. No really, I never heard it.

POET. Don't you ever go to the theater?

MISS. Oh, yes — I was at the opera only the other day with — you know, with one of my friends and her uncle, to hear Cavalleria Rusticana.

POET. Hm, you don't go then to see plays.

MISS. I never get tickets for them.

POET. I'll send you a ticket soon.

MISS.   Oh, do! And don't forget it. But for something funny.

POET.   Oh . . . something funny . . . you don't care to see anything sad?

MISS.   Not very much.

POET.   Not even if it is a play of mine.

MISS.   A play of yours? Do you write for the theater?

POET.   Let me light a candle now. I haven't seen you since you have become my best beloved — Angel! (*He lights a candle*)

MISS.   Don't. I'm ashamed. Give me a cover at least.

POET.   Later! (*He approaches her with the light, and looks at her a long while*)

MISS.   (*Covering her face with her hands*) Go away, Robert!

POET.   You are beautiful, you are Beauty itself. You are Nature herself. You are the simplicity which is holy.

MISS.   Ouch! You are dropping wax on me. Look, why aren't you more careful?

POET.   (*Puts the candle away*) You are that for which I have long sought. You love me for my own sake. You would love me even if I were only a counter-jumper. That's balm to one's heart. I must confess I was suspicious until this moment. Tell me, honestly, you didn't have any notion that I am Biebitz?

MISS.   Oh, pshaw, I don't even know what you are talking about. I never heard of any Biebitz.

POET.   What is fame! No, forget what I have told you. Forget even the name. I am Robert and I want to remain Robert to you. I was only joking. (*Lightly*) I am not a writer at all. I'm a clerk, and in the evening I play the piano in a dance-hall.

MISS.   But now I'm all mixed up . . . and the way you look at one. What is the matter, yes, what do you mean?

POET.   It is very strange — something that has never happened to me, sweetheart; I am on the verge of tears. You move me deeply. We ought to live together. Will you? We will be very much in love with each other.

MISS.   Is it true about the dance-hall?

POET.   Yes, but don't ask any more about it. If you love me, don't ask me anything. Tell me, can't you get away for a few weeks?

MISS.   How do you mean get away?

POET.   Well, I mean, leave home?

MISS.   How absurd! How could I! What would mother say? And without me everything would be topsy-turvy at home in no time.

POET.   It would be so wonderful to live with you a few weeks, all alone with you, somewhere far away, in the forest, in the world of nature . . . Nature. And then, some day, "Good-by" — each going, without the other knowing where.

MISS. You are talking already about saying good-by. And I thought that you loved me such a lot.

POET. That is just the reason — (*Bends over her, and kisses her upon the forehead*) You sweet darling!

MISS. Please, hold me tight. I feel so cold.

POET. I fancy it's time for you to dress. Wait, I'll light a few more candles for you.

MISS. (*Rising*) Don't look this way.

POET. No. (*At the window*) Tell me, child, are you happy?

MISS. What do you mean?

POET. I mean are you happy the way things are in general?

MISS. Well, they might be better.

POET. You misunderstand me. You have told me enough about your conditions at home. I know you are not a princess. Leaving all that aside, do you feel alive? Do you feel life pulsing through you?

MISS. Come, have you a comb?

POET. (*Goes to the dressing-table, hands her a comb, and watches her*) Good Lord, how lovely you look!

MISS. Please . . . don't!

POET. Please, stay a while yet. I'll get something for supper, and . . .

MISS. But it is awfully late already.

POET. It is not yet nine.

MISS. Dear me, I must hurry. Please!

POET. When shall I see you again?

MISS. When would you like to see me?

POET. To-morrow.

MISS. What day is to-morrow?

POET. Saturday.

MISS. Oh, then I can't. I must take my little sister to her guardian.

POET. Then Sunday . . . hm . . . Sunday . . . on Sunday . . . now I'll have to explain something to you. — I'm not Biebitz, but Biebitz is a friend of mine. I'll introduce him to you sometime. Biebitz's play will be given Sunday. I'll send you tickets, and take you home after the performance. You will tell me then how you liked the play. Won't you?

MISS. Here you are talking about this Biebitz again. — I don't understand what it is all about.

POET. I won't know you really, until I know what impression the play made on you.

MISS. Now . . . I'm ready.

POET. Come, sweetheart. (*They go out*)

The Poet and the Actress

A room in an inn in the country. It is an evening in spring; moonlight floods the meadows and hills; the windows are open. A deep silence reigns. The POET *and the* ACTRESS *enter, and as they cross the threshold, the candle which the* POET *is carrying in his hand is blown out.*

POET. Oh. . . .

ACTRESS. What's the matter?

POET. The candle.—But we don't need any. Look, how light it is. Wonderful!

ACTRESS. (*Sinks suddenly down at the window with her hands folded*)

POET. What's the matter with you?

ACTRESS. (*Remains silent*)

POET. (*Going to her*) What are you doing?

ACTRESS. (*Indignant*) Can't you see that I am praying?—

POET. Do you believe in God?

ACTRESS. Of course I do; I am not a fool.

POET. Oh, I see!

ACTRESS. Come, kneel down beside me. It will do you good to pray just once. None of the gems will drop out of your crown.

POET. (*Kneels beside her, and puts his arm around her waist*)

ACTRESS. Libertine!—(*Rises*) And do you know to whom I prayed?

POET. To God, I suppose.

ACTRESS. (*With deep sarcasm*) Oh, of course! It was to you to whom I prayed.

POET. Then why did you look out of the window?

ACTRESS. Tell me rather where you have lured me.

POET. But, child, it was your idea. You wanted to go to the country— and picked out this very place.

ACTRESS. Well, wasn't I right?

POET. Certainly. It's charming here. When you consider that we are just two hours from Vienna—complete solitude. And delightful scenery!

ACTRESS. Isn't it? If you had any real talent, this place might inspire you to write.

POET. Have you been here before?

ACTRESS. Have I been here before? Indeed I have! I have lived here for years.

POET. With whom?

ACTRESS. With Dick, of course.

POET. Oh, really!

ACTRESS. How I adored that man! —

POET. You've told me all about that already.

ACTRESS. I am sorry — I can go away again, if I bore you!

POET. You bore me? . . . You can't imagine what you mean to me. . . . You are a whole world in itself. . . . You are divine, you are a genius. . . . You are the simplicity which is holy. . . . Yes, you. . . . But you oughtn't to talk about Dick now.

ACTRESS. That was merely a slip! Well! —

POET. I am glad that you feel that way.

ACTRESS. Come, give me a kiss!

POET. (*Kisses her*)

ACTRESS. But now we had better say good-night. Good-night, darling!

POET. What do you mean by that?

ACTRESS. I mean, I am going to lie down and go to sleep.

POET. Yes, — that's very well, but when it comes to saying "good-night". . . . where do I sleep?

ACTRESS. There are surely a lot of other rooms in this house.

POET. But they don't appeal to me. Don't you think I had better light a candle now?

ACTRESS. Yes.

POET. (*Lights a candle, which stands upon the dressing-table*) What a charming room . . . and what pious people they must be. Pictures of saints everywhere. . . . It would be interesting to spend some time among people like this . . . quite another world. How little we know of the lives of others!

ACTRESS. Don't talk nonsense, but just give me the bag from the table.

POET. Here, beloved!

ACTRESS. (*Takes a small framed picture out of the handbag and puts it on the dressing-table*)

POET. What's that?

ACTRESS. That's the Virgin.

POET. Do you always carry her around with you?

ACTRESS. She is my talisman. And now go, Robert!

POET. You are joking? Can't I help you?

ACTRESS. No, you must go now.

POET.   And when may I return?

ACTRESS.   In ten minutes.

POET.   (*Kisses her*) Au revoir!

ACTRESS.   Where will you go?

POET.   I shall walk up and down under your window. I love to wander about outdoors at night time. My finest inspirations come to me that way. And especially near you, under the breath of your longing, I might call it . . . entwined in your art.

ACTRESS.   You talk like an idiot. . . .

POET.   (*Hurt*) There are women who might say . . . like a poet.

ACTRESS.   Oh, well, but do go now. But don't start to flirt with the waitress. —

POET.   (*Goes*)

ACTRESS.   (*Undresses. She hears the* POET *going down the wooden stairway, and, then hears his footsteps below her window. As soon as she is undressed, she goes to the window and looks down to where he stands waiting. She calls to him in a whisper*) Come!

POET.   (*Comes quickly upstairs and runs toward her. She in the meantime has gone to bed, and extinguished the light. He locks the door*)

ACTRESS.   So, now you may sit down beside me, and tell me a story.

POET.   (*Sits down on the bed beside her*) Hadn't I better close the window? Isn't it too cold for you?

ACTRESS.   Oh, no!

POET.   Now, what shall I tell you?

ACTRESS.   Tell me to whom you are unfaithful at this moment?

POET.   I'm sorry, I'm not unfaithful yet.

ACTRESS.   Well, if it's any satisfaction to you, I am unfaithful to some one too.

POET.   So I can imagine.

ACTRESS.   And who do you suppose it is?

POET.   But, child, how do you expect me to know?

ACTRESS.   Guess, then.

POET.   Wait . . . your manager.

ACTRESS.   My dear man, I'm not a chorus-girl.

POET.   Well, I am only guessing.

ACTRESS.   Guess again.

POET.   Then it's your leading-man . . . Benno —

ACTRESS.   Nonsense! He doesn't care for women at all . . . didn't you know that? He carries on with his postman!

POET.   No, really! —

ACTRESS.   Now come, kiss me.

POET.   (*Embraces her*)

ACTRESS.   But what are you doing?

POET.   Why do you torment me so?

ACTRESS.   Listen, Robert, I have a suggestion to make to you. Come lie down in bed with me.

POET.   I accept.

ACTRESS.   Come quickly, come quickly!

POET.   Yes . . . if I had had my way, I would have been there long ago. . . . Listen. . . .

ACTRESS.   What?

POET.   The crickets are chirping outside.

ACTRESS.   You are crazy, child, there are no crickets here.

POET.   But surely you hear them.

ACTRESS.   Hurry up.

POET.   (*Beside her*) Here I am.

ACTRESS.   Now lie quite still. . . . Sh . . . don't move. . . .

POET.   Yes, but why?

ACTRESS.   You would rather like to have an affair with me?

POET.   I should think that's obvious by now.

ACTRESS.   There are many who would like that. . . .

POET.   But it would seem that at the moment the odds are on my side. . . .

ACTRESS.   Then, come, my cricket! I shall call you "cricket" from now on.

POET.   All right. . . .

ACTRESS.   Now, tell me, whom am I deceiving?

POET.   Whom? . . . Perhaps me. . . .

ACTRESS.   Child, you have softening of the brain.

POET.   Or some one . . . some one whom you have never seen . . . some one, whom you don't even know, some one — who is predestined for you and whom you will never find. . . .

ACTRESS.   Please don't talk such magnificent nonsense.

POET.   . . . Isn't it strange . . . you too — and yet one could think. — But no, it would destroy the best in you, if one should . . . come, come — come. —

*   *   *

ACTRESS.   That's better than acting in idiotic plays. . . . Don't you think so?

POET.   Well, it seems to me, that it is a good thing you sometimes have to act in an intelligent one.

ACTRESS.   You conceited puppy. I suppose you are thinking of one of your own plays again.

POET.   Yes, I am.

ACTRESS.   (*Seriously*) It is really a splendid play!

POET.   Well, then!

ACTRESS.   You are a great genius, Robert!

POET.   And you might also tell me now why you didn't turn up the day before yesterday. There was absolutely nothing the matter with you.

ACTRESS.   Well, I wanted to annoy you.

POET.   But why? What have I done to you? —

ACTRESS.   You were over-bearing.

POET.   In what way?

ACTRESS.   Everybody at the theater thinks you are.

POET.   Really.

ACTRESS.   But I told them, he has a perfect right to be over-bearing.

POET.   And what did they say?

ACTRESS.   What could they say? I am not on speaking terms with any of them. ·

POET.   Oh, I see.

ACTRESS.   They would like nothing better than to poison me, every one of them. But they won't succeed.

POET.   Don't think now of others. Let's be happy that we are here together, and tell me that you love me.

ACTRESS.   What further proof can you want?

POET.   It's a thing that can't be proven anyway.

ACTRESS.   I like that! What else do you want?

POET.   How many are there that you have tried to convince in this way . . . did you love all of them?

ACTRESS.   No, I have loved only one.

POET.   (*Embraces her*) My. . . .

ACTRESS.   Dick.

POET.   My name is Robert. What can I mean to you, if you are thinking of Dick, now?

ACTRESS.   You are a mood of mine.

POET.   I am pleased to know it.

ACTRESS.   Well, tell me, aren't you proud?

POET.   Why should I be proud?

ACTRESS.   It seems to me that you have good reason to be.

POET.   Oh, because of that.

ACTRESS.   Yes, because of that, my little cricket! — What about the chirping? Are they still chirping?

POET.   All the time. Don't you hear them?

ACTRESS.   Of course, I hear them. But, child, those are frogs.

POET.   You are wrong. Frogs croak.

ACTRESS.   Of course, they croak.

POET.   But this is not croaking, child, this is chirping.

ACTRESS.   You are about the most stubborn person I have ever met. Kiss me, froggie.

POET.   Please don't call me that. It gets on my nerves.

ACTRESS.   Well, what shall I call you?

POET.   My name is Robert.

ACTRESS.   Oh, but that's stupid.

POET.   But won't you please call me simply by my own name?

ACTRESS.   Well, then, Robert, give me a kiss. . . . Ah! (*She kisses him*) Now, are you satisfied, froggie?

POET.   May I light a cigarette?

ACTRESS.   Give me one too. (*He takes his cigarette-case from the dressing-table; takes two cigarettes out; lights both, and gives her one*) By the way, you haven't said a word about my performance yesterday.

POET.   What performance?

ACTRESS.   Well.

POET.   Oh, yes. I wasn't at the theater.

ACTRESS.   You are joking.

POET.   Not in the least. When you didn't turn up the day before, I assumed you hadn't fully recovered yesterday, and so I decided not to go.

ACTRESS.   You missed something wonderful.

POET.   Yes.

ACTRESS.   It was a sensation. The people actually grew pale.

POET.   You saw that?

ACTRESS.   Benno said: Child, you acted divinely.

POET.   Hm! . . . And so ill the day before.

ACTRESS.   Indeed I was. And do you know why? Because I felt such a longing for you.

POET.   A little while ago you said that you stayed away just to annoy me.

ACTRESS.   But what do you know about my love for you? Everything leaves you cold. And I have been delirious for nights. In a high fever — hundred and four degrees.

POET.   Rather high for a mood.

ACTRESS.   You call that a mood? I am dying for love of you, and you call it a mood — ?

POET.   And Dick. . . ?

ACTRESS.   Dick? . . . Don't talk to me about that galley-slave! —

The Actress and the Count

The bedroom of the ACTRESS, *luxuriously furnished. It is midday. The curtains are still down; a candle is burning on the dressing-table. The* ACTRESS *is disclosed in her four-poster bed. Many newspapers are strewn about on the cover. The* COUNT *in the uniform of a captain of the Dragoons enters. He remains standing at the door.*

ACTRESS. Ah, Count.

COUNT. Your mother said I might, otherwise I would not—

ACTRESS. Please, come closer.

COUNT. I kiss your hand. Pardon me—when you come in from the street . . . I can't see a thing yet. So . . . here we are (*at her bed*). I kiss your hand.

ACTRESS. Please sit down, Count.

COUNT. Your mother said, My daughter isn't well. . . . Nothing serious, I hope.

ACTRESS. Nothing serious? I was on the verge of death.

COUNT. Oh, dear, oh, dear, is it possible?

ACTRESS. It is very good of you to have taken the trouble to call.

COUNT. On the verge of death! And only last night you acted divinely.

ACTRESS. It was a great triumph, wasn't it?

COUNT. Tremendous! . . . The audience was carried away. I won't say anything about myself.

ACTRESS. Thanks, for the beautiful flowers.

COUNT. Nothing at all, Mademoiselle.

ACTRESS. (*Indicating with her eyes a large flower-basket, which stands on a little table near the window*) There they are.

COUNT. You were literally overwhelmed with flowers and wreaths yesterday.

ACTRESS. They are still in my dressing-room. All I brought home was your flowers.

COUNT. (*Kissing her hand*) How sweet of you.

49

ACTRESS. (*Suddenly seizes his hand, and kisses it*)

COUNT. But, Mademoiselle.

ACTRESS. Don't be frightened, Count, it doesn't put you under any obligations.

COUNT. You are a strange being . . . a sort of a problem almost— (*Pause*)

ACTRESS. Miss Birken, I suppose, is much less of a problem.

COUNT. That little lady isn't a problem at all, although . . . I really know her only very slightly.

ACTRESS. Oh!

COUNT. That's the actual truth. But you are a problem. I've always had a yearning for a problem. It's really been a deep personal loss to me, that until yesterday. . . . I *never* saw you act.

ACTRESS. Really?

COUNT. Yes! You see, going to the theater is so complicated. I am used to dining late . . . then when I get there, the best part of the play is over. Isn't that true?

ACTRESS. From now on, I suppose, you will dine earlier.

COUNT. I've thought of that too. Or maybe I won't dine at all. Dining isn't a special pleasure anyhow.

ACTRESS. Are there any pleasures left to an old man like you?

COUNT. That's a question I often ask myself. But I am not an old man. There must be some other reason.

ACTRESS. Do you think so?

COUNT. Yes. Bobby, for instance, says, that I am a philosopher. You know he means that I do too much thinking.

ACTRESS. Yes . . . thinking is a misfortune.

COUNT. I have too much time, that's why I reflect. You see, I've often thought if they would transfer me to Vienna, things would be better. There's diversion here, stimulation. But at the bottom, it's not really very different from up there.

ACTRESS. What do you mean by "up there"?

COUNT. Well, down there, you know, in Hungary, in the God forsaken country towns, where I've been stationed most of the time.

ACTRESS. And what did you do in Hungary?

COUNT. Well, as I am telling you, military service.

ACTRESS. Yes, but why did you stay in Hungary so long?

COUNT. Oh, things happen that way.

ACTRESS. But it must be enough to drive one mad.

COUNT. But why? You have a lot more work there, than here. You know, drilling recruits, breaking in mounts . . . and the country really isn't as bad as they say. They are really quite beautiful, the lowlands — and marvelous sunsets. Too bad I'm not a painter, I've often thought if I were, I would paint them. We had a young chap, Splany, in our regiment, who could do it. — But, dear me, what dull stories I am telling you.

ACTRESS.   Please go on; they are delightful!

COUNT.   Do you know, the nice thing about you is the way one can chat with you, Bobby told me all about it. And it's so seldom one can find any one like that.

ACTRESS.   Down there in Hungary, I suppose.

COUNT.   But it's quite the same in Vienna! People are always the same. Where there are more of them, the crowd is larger. That's the whole difference. Tell me, do you really like people?

ACTRESS.   Like them — ? I hate them! I hate to look at them. I never see any one. I'm always alone. Nobody enters my house.

COUNT.   You see, I sort of thought that you hated people. It must often be the case with artists. If one lives in the higher regions. . . . Well, you are lucky, you know at least why you live!

ACTRESS.   Who told you that? I haven't the slightest notion what I'm living for!

COUNT.   But really — to be famous — to be fêted —

ACTRESS.   Does that mean happiness?

COUNT.   Happiness? There really is no such thing as happiness. All the things that people talk about most, don't exist . . . for instance, love. That's one of them.

ACTRESS.   I suppose you are right.

COUNT.   Enjoyment . . . intoxication . . . very good, nobody can deny them . . . they are something real. Now, when I am enjoying myself . . . very good, I am aware that I am enjoying myself. Or I am intoxicated, good. That also is something real. And when it's over, well then it's over.

ACTRESS.   (*Grandly*) It is over.

COUNT.   But as soon as one does not, how shall I express it, as soon as one does not give oneself up to the moment, I mean, if one thinks of the future or the past . . . well, everything is over in a moment. . . . Afterwards . . . there is sadness . . . before . . . there is uncertainty . . . in a word, one only becomes confused. Isn't that so?

ACTRESS.   (*Nods with wide open eyes*) It seems, you have grasped the essence of things.

COUNT.   And, you see, when you have once clearly grasped this, it really doesn't matter whether you live in Vienna or in the Puszta[1] or in Steinamanger.[2] You see, for instance . . . where may I put my cap? Yes, thank you . . . what were we talking about?

---

[1] A monotonous, treeless region in the great plain of Hungary.
[2] A provincial town in Hungary about 60 miles south of Vienna.

ACTRESS. About the Puszta.

COUNT. Of course. Well, as I said, there isn't much difference, whether I spend the evening in the officers' mess or at the club. It's all the same.

ACTRESS. And what about love?

COUNT. If you believe in it, some one will always be there who will love you.

ACTRESS. Like Miss Birken, for example.

COUNT. I really don't see why you always have to come back to that little lady.

ACTRESS. But she's your mistress, isn't she?

COUNT. Who says so?

ACTRESS. Everybody knows it.

COUNT. Except myself, strange to say.

ACTRESS. But you fought a duel on her account!

COUNT. Maybe. I was even killed without my knowing it.

ACTRESS. You are a gentleman, won't you sit closer to me?

COUNT. With pleasure.

ACTRESS. Here. (*She draws him to her, and passes her hand through his hair*) I knew you would come to-day.

COUNT. How did you know?

ACTRESS. I knew it last night in the theater.

COUNT. You saw me from the stage, then?

ACTRESS. But man alive! Didn't you notice that I acted for you alone?

COUNT. No, really?

ACTRESS. I was as on wings, when I saw you sitting in the first row.

COUNT. As on wings? On my account? I hadn't the slightest suspicion that you noticed me!

ACTRESS. Your aristocratic reserve is enough to drive one to despair.

COUNT. But . . .

ACTRESS. "But"! . . . At least, take your saber off!

COUNT. If you permit. (*Takes it off, and leans it against the bed*)

ACTRESS. And now give me a kiss.

COUNT. (*Kisses her, she clings to him*)

ACTRESS. It wculd have been better if I had never seen you.

COUNT. But this seems better to me.

ACTRESS. Count, you are a poseur!

COUNT. I — why?

ACTRESS. Can't you imagine how happy many a man would be if he were in your place!

COUNT. I'm perfectly happy.

ACTRESS.   Well, I thought happiness didn't exist. Why do you look at me that way? I believe you are afraid of me, Count!

COUNT.   I told you, Mademoiselle, you are a problem.

ACTRESS.   Oh, don't bother me with your philosophy . . . come to me. And ask me for anything at all . . . you can have whatever you want. You are so handsome.

COUNT.   Well then, may I ask (*kissing her hand*) that I may call again this evening?

ACTRESS.   This evening . . . but I have to act then.

COUNT.   After the play.

ACTRESS.   And you ask for nothing else?

COUNT.   I shall ask for everything else after the play.

ACTRESS.   (*Hurt*) You can beg a long while then, you abominable poseur.

COUNT.   But, see, we've been perfectly frank with each other so far . . . it seems to me it would be so much more beautiful after the play . . . much cozier than now, when . . . I have a sort of feeling the door might open any moment. . . .

ACTRESS.   It does not open from the outside.

COUNT.   Well, you see, I have an idea one shouldn't lightly spoil in advance something which may be very beautiful.

ACTRESS.   Possibly! . . .

COUNT.   To tell the truth, love in the morning seems rather horrible to me.

ACTRESS.   Well — you are about the worst case of lunacy I have ever met!

COUNT.   I am not talking about women in general . . . because in general it doesn't make any difference anyway. But women like you . . . no, you may call me a fool a hundred times over. But women like you . . . one doesn't take them before breakfast. And so . . . you know . . . so . . .

ACTRESS.   Oh, but you are a darling!

COUNT.   You understand, what I have said, don't you? I sort of imagine it like. . . .

ACTRESS.   How do you imagine it?

COUNT.   Like this. . . . I wait for you in a carriage after the play, then we drive somewhere for supper —

ACTRESS.   I am not Miss Birken.

COUNT.   I didn't mean to say you were. Only, it seems to me, you have to be in the right sort of mood for everything. In my case the mood doesn't come until supper. The most beautiful thing of all is when we drive home together, and then . . .

ACTRESS.   And then?

COUNT.   And then . . . well, that depends upon circumstances.

ACTRESS.   Do sit closer. Closer.

COUNT.   (*Sitting down on the bed*) Seems to me, that out of the pillows comes a fragrance . . . mignonette — isn't it?

ACTRESS.   It's very warm in here, don't you think so?

COUNT.   (*Bends down, and kisses her neck*)

ACTRESS.   Oh, Count, that is contrary to your program.

COUNT.   Who said anything about "program." I never have any program.

ACTRESS.   (*Drawing him close to her*)

COUNT.   It really is very warm.

ACTRESS.   Do you think so? And so dark, just as if it were evening. . . . (*Draws him toward her*) It is evening . . . it is night. . . . Close your eyes, if there is too much light for you. Come! . . . Come! . . .

COUNT.   (*Offers no further resistance*)

*   *   *

ACTRESS.   And what about atmosphere now, you poseur?

COUNT.   You are a little devil.

ACTRESS.   What a thing to say!

COUNT.   Well, then an angel.

ACTRESS.   You should have been an actor! Really! You understand women! And do you know, what I shall do now?

COUNT.   Well?

ACTRESS.   I shall tell you that I shall never see you again.

COUNT.   But why?

ACTRESS.   Never, never. You are too dangerous! You would drive a woman mad. Here you are standing before me, as though nothing had happened.

COUNT.   But . . .

ACTRESS.   Please remember, Count, I have just given you everything.

COUNT.   I shall never forget it!

ACTRESS.   And what about to-night?

COUNT.   What do you mean?

ACTRESS.   Well — you wanted to wait for me after the theater?

COUNT.   Oh, yes, let's say, the day after to-morrow.

ACTRESS.   What do you mean by "the day after to-morrow"? We were talking about to-day.

COUNT.   There wouldn't be much sense in that.

ACTRESS.   Old man!

COUNT.   You don't quite understand me. What I mean has rather to do, how shall I express myself, rather concerns the soul.

ACTRESS.   What concern of mine is your soul?

COUNT.   Believe me, it has much to do with it. It seems all wrong to me, this notion, that you can separate the two.

ACTRESS.   Don't bother me with your philosophy. If I want any of that, I can read books.

COUNT.   One never learns from books.

ACTRESS.   Very true! And that's why you ought to wait for me to-night. As to the soul, we will come to some sort of an understanding, you villain!

COUNT.   Well, then, if I may, I shall wait in my carriage. . . .

ACTRESS.   You shall wait for me here in my home —

COUNT.   . . . After the play.

ACTRESS.   Of course. (*He buckles on his sword*)

ACTRESS.   What are you doing?

COUNT.   It seems to me it is time for me to go. For a formal call I have stayed a bit too long as it is.

ACTRESS.   Well, this evening it shall be a formal call.

COUNT.   Do you think so?

ACTRESS.   I'll take care of that. And now give me a last kiss, you darling little philosopher. Here, you seducer, you . . . sweet child, you seller of souls, you . . . panther. (*After she has ardently kissed him several times, she thrusts him violently away*) Count, you have done me a great honor.

COUNT.   Not at all, mademoiselle! (*At the door*) Au revoir.

ACTRESS.   Good-by, and love to Steinamanger.

The Count and the Girl of the Streets

It is morning toward six o'clock. A poorly furnished room with on
window. The dirty yellowish blinds are down. Tattered, greenish curtain
On the dresser are several photographs, and beside them a cheap woman
hat of conspicuously bad taste. Behind the mirror are cheap Japanes
fans. On the table over which is drawn a reddish cover is an oil-lamp. It
burning low with a disagreeable odor, and has a shade of yellow pape
Beside it is a pitcher with remains of beer, and a half-empty glass. — O
the floor beside the bed a woman's clothes are lying in disorder. They loo
as though they had just been quickly thrown off. The GIRL *lies sleeping i*
the bed, breathing quietly. The COUNT *is lying on the sofa fully dresse*
with his light overcoat on. His hat lies on the floor at the head of the sof

COUNT. (*Stirs, rubs his eyes, sits up suddenly, remains seated, and look*
around) Where am I? . . . Oh, yes . . . I actually went home with th
woman, it seems. . . . (*He rises quickly, notices her bed*) Oh, there sh
is. . . . Queer, what sort of things can happen, even at my age.
haven't the faintest notion, did they carry me up here? No. . . .
remember — coming into the room. . . . I was still awake then, o
waked up . . . or . . . or maybe it's only the room that reminds o
something? . . . 'Pon my soul, yes, of course . . . it was yesterday I sa
it. . . . (*Looks at his watch*) What! yesterday, a couple of hours ago! –
But, I knew, that something had to happen . . . I felt it in my bones . .
when I began to drink yesterday, I felt that . . . and what has hap
pened? . . . Nothing. . . . Or did there. . . ? 'Pon my soul . . . for . . . fo
ten years it hasn't happened to me that I don't know. . . . Well, let's b
honest at any rate, I was drunk. . . . If I only knew since when . . .
remember perfectly when Bobby and I went into the all-night café
and . . . no, no. . . . We left together . . . and then on the way. . . . Ye
that's it, Bobby and I rode in my carriage. . . . But, why do I worry m
brains about it? It doesn't really matter. Let's see that we get out o
here. (*Rises. The lamp shakes*) Oh! (*Looks at the sleeping* GIRL) Wel
she sleeps the sleep of the just. I don't remember anything — but I'

56

put the money on the table . . . and then, good-by. . . . (*He stands in front of her, and looks at her for a considerable time*) If I didn't know what she is! (*Studies her*) I've known many who didn't look as virtuous even in their sleep. 'Pon my soul. . . . Bobby would say again, I'm philosophizing, but the truth is, sleep makes all equal, so it seems to me — like its brother, death. . . . Hm, I should like to know, whether. . . . No, I'd remember that. . . . No, no, I dropped like a log on the sofa right away . . . and nothing happened. . . . It is unbelievable how much alike all women sometimes look. . . . Well, let's go (*He is about to go*) Oh, of course. (*He takes his wallet, and is about to take out a banknote*)

GIRL.   (*Awakening*) Well . . . who's there so early in the morning — ? (*Recognizing him*) Good morning, sonny!

COUNT.   Good morning. Have a good sleep?

GIRL.   (*Stretching*) Oh, come here. Give me a little kiss.

COUNT.   (*Bends down to her, considers, and draws back*) I was just going. . . .

GIRL.   Going?

COUNT.   It's really about time.

GIRL.   You want to go away?

COUNT.   (*Half-embarrassed*) Well. . . .

GIRL.   Well, good-by, you'll come some other time.

COUNT.   Yes, good-by. But, won't you give me your hand?

GIRL.   (*Reaches out her hand from under the cover*)

COUNT.   (*Takes her hand, and kisses it mechanically, and becoming aware of it, he smiles*) Just as with a princess. Besides, if one only. . . .

GIRL.   Why do you look at me that way?

COUNT.   If one only sees the head, as now . . . anyway, each and every one looks innocent when she first awakes . . . 'Pon my soul, one might imagine almost anything, if the kerosene didn't smell so. . . .

GIRL.   Yes, the lamps are always a nuisance.

COUNT.   How old are you really?

GIRL.   Well, what would you guess?

COUNT.   Twenty-four.

GIRL.   Oh, of course!

COUNT.   Older?

GIRL.   I'm not yet twenty.

COUNT.   And how long have you been . . .

GIRL.   A year.

COUNT.   You began early.

GIRL.   Better too early, than too late.

COUNT.   (*Sits down upon her bed*) Tell me, are you really happy?

GIRL.   Am I, what?

COUNT. I mean, are things going well with you?

GIRL. Oh, things always go well with me.

COUNT. Yes. . . . Well, did it never occur to you that you might become something else?

GIRL. What might I become?

COUNT. Well. . . . You are a very pretty girl. You might take a lover, for example.

GIRL. Do you imagine I haven't any?

COUNT. Yes, I know that — But I mean just one single one, who would take care of you, so that you wouldn't have to go with everybody.

GIRL. I don't go with everybody. Thank heaven, I don't have to. I pick those I want.

COUNT. (*Looks around the room*)

GIRL. (*Noticing it*) We move downtown next month, to the Spiegelgasse.

COUNT. We? Who?

GIRL. Well, the Madam, and the couple of other girls who live here.

COUNT. There are others —

GIRL. Next door . . . don't you hear? . . . that is Milly. She was in the café too.

COUNT. I hear some one snoring.

GIRL. That's Milly. She will snore the whole day long until ten o'clock to-night. Then she gets up, and goes to the café.

COUNT. What an awful life!

GIRL. Of course it is. It annoys the Madam a lot. I'm always on the streets by noon.

COUNT. What do you do on the streets at noon?

GIRL. What do you suppose I do? I'm going on my beat then.

COUNT. Oh, yes . . . of course. . . . (*Rises, takes out his wallet, and puts a banknote on the table*) Good-by!

GIRL. Going already. . . . Good-by. . . . Call again soon. (*Turns on her side*)

COUNT. (*Stands still*) Tell me, is everything a matter of indifference to you already?

GIRL. What?

COUNT. I mean, don't you get pleasure out of anything any more?

GIRL. (*Yawning*) I want to sleep.

COUNT. It's all the same to you whether he is young or old or whether he . . .

GIRL. Why do you ask?

COUNT. . . . Well (*Suddenly hitting upon a thought*) 'pon my soul, now I know of whom you remind me, it's . . .

GIRL. Do I look like some one?

COUNT. Unbelievable, unbelievable. Now please, don't talk, at least not for a minute.... (*Looking at her*) The very same features (*He kisses her suddenly on the eyes*), the very image.

GIRL. Well....

COUNT. 'Pon my soul, it's too bad that you ... aren't something different.... You could make your fortune!

GIRL. You talk just like Frank.

COUNT. Who is Frank?

GIRL. The waiter in our café.

COUNT. In what way am I just like Frank?

GIRL. He is also always telling me I might make my fortune, and wanting me to marry him.

COUNT. Why don't you?

GIRL. No thank you.... I don't want to marry, no, not for any price.... Later on, perhaps.

COUNT. The eyes ... the very same eyes.... Bobby would surely call me a fool. — But I must kiss your eyes once more ... so ... and now God bless you, now I must go.

GIRL. Good-by....

COUNT. (*At the door*) Tell me ... aren't you a bit surprised? ...

GIRL. At what?

COUNT. That I don't want anything of you.

GIRL. There are many men who aren't in the mood in the morning.

COUNT. Of course ... (*To himself*) Absurd, that I expect to be surprised.... Well, good-by.... (*He is near the door*) But really, I'm disappointed. I ought to know that women like her care only about money ... what am I saying ... it is beautiful, that at least she doesn't pretend; should make one glad ... (*Aloud*) Do you know, I shall come to see you again soon?

GIRL. (*With closed eyes*) All right.

COUNT. When are you at home?

GIRL. I'm always at home. You only have to ask for Leocadia.

COUNT. Leocadia.... All right — Well, God bless you. (*At the door*) The wine is still in my head. But after all it is sublime.... I am with a woman like her and haven't done anything but kiss her eyes, because she reminded me of some one.... (*Turns toward her*) Tell me, Leocadia, does it often happen that any one leaves you in this way?

GIRL. What way?

COUNT. As I do.

GIRL. In the morning?

COUNT. No ... have you ever had any one with you, — who didn't want anything of you?

GIRL. No, that has never happened to me.

COUNT.   Well, what do you think then? Do you think I didn't like you?

GIRL.   Why shouldn't you like me? You liked me well enough by night.

COUNT.   I like you now, too.

GIRL.   But you liked me better last night.

COUNT.   What makes you think that?

GIRL.   Why ask such foolish questions?

COUNT.   Last night . . . well, tell me, didn't I drop right down on the sofa?

GIRL.   Certainly . . . with me.

COUNT.   With you?

GIRL.   Yes, don't you remember?

COUNT.   I did . . . both of us. . . .

GIRL.   But you fell asleep right away.

COUNT.   Right away. . . . So . . . that's what happened? . . .

GIRL.   Yes, sonny. But you must have been terribly drunk, that you don't remember.

COUNT.   So. . . . And yet . . . there is a faint resemblance. . . . Good-by. . . . (*Listens*) . . . What is the matter?

GIRL.   The servant is up. Give her a tip as you go out. The outside door is open, so you won't have to give anything to the janitor.

COUNT.   (*In the anteroom*) Well. . . . It would have been beautiful, if I had kissed her only on the eyes. It would have been almost an adventure. . . . But it wasn't my destiny. (*The servant opens the door*) Ah—here. . . . Good-night.—

SERVANT.   Good morning!

COUNT.   Of course . . . good morning . . . good morning.